CONCILIUM

Religion in the Eighties

CONCILIUM

Editorial Directors

General Secretariat: Prins Bernhardstraat 2, 6521 AB Nijmegen, The Netherlands

Concilium 179 (3/1985): Moral Theology

CONCILIUM

List of Members

Advisory Committee: Moral Theology

Directors:

Dietmar Mieth	Tübingen	West Germany
Jacques Pohier OP	Paris	France

Members:

Franz Böckle	Bonn	West Germany
Klaus Demmer	Rome	Italy
Ignacio Ellacuría	Managua	Nicaragua
Margaret Farley	New Haven, Conn.	USA
Erich Fuchs	Lausanne/Geneva	Switzerland
Josef Fuchs SJ	Rome	Italy
Gérard Gilleman SJ	Delhi	India
Tullo Goffi	Brescia	Italy
Léonce Hamelin OFN	Montreal	Canada
Bernard Häring CSsR	Rome	Italy
Benedicta Hintersberger	Augsburg	West Germany
Antonio Hortelano	Rome/Madrid	Italy/Spain
Helmut Juros	Warsaw	Poland
Walter Kerber SJ	Munich	West Germany
Harry Kuitert	Amstelveen	The Netherlands
Richard McCormick SJ	Washington, DC	USA
Enda McDonagh	Maynooth	Ireland
Helen Oppenheimer	Jersey	Channel Islands
Bernard Quelquejeu OP	Paris	France
Warren Reich	Washington, DC	USA
René Simon	Paris	France
Jaime Snoek CSSR	Juiz de Fora	Brazil
José Solozábal	Bilbao	Spain
Paul Sporken	Maastricht	The Netherlands
Xavier Thévénot	Paris	France
Marciano Vidal	Madrid	Spain

SUICIDE
AND
THE RIGHT TO DIE

Edited by
Jacques Pohier
and
Dietmar Mieth

English Language Editor
Marcus Lefébure

T. & T. CLARK LTD
Edinburgh

June 1985
T. & T. Clark Ltd, 36 George Street, Edinburgh EH2 2LQ
ISBN: 0 567 30059 5

ISSN: 0010-5236

Typeset by C. R. Barber & Partners (Highlands) Ltd, Fort William
Printed by Page Brothers (Norwich) Ltd

Concilium: Published February, April, June, August, October, December.
Subscriptions 1985: UK: £19.95 (including postage and packing); USA: US$40.00
(including air mail postage and packing); Canada: Canadian$50.00 (including air mail
postage and packing); other countries: £19.95 (including postage and packing).

CONTENTS

vii

Part II
Theological Reflection

Editorial

'900,000 PEOPLE are under imminent threat of death in Ethiopia', writes the newspaper *Le Monde* (Thursday, 22 November 1984, p. 30). '30 million children live on the streets in Brazil, a quarter of them abandoned by their parents' (*ibid.*, Wednesday, 21 November, p. 1). Each day any reader of *Concilium* can find facts like these in his daily paper. One day he/she may learn that Mao Tse Tung's 'great leap forward' resulted in tens of millions of deaths. Another day, that 150 million people are threatened by famine in Africa. And on another, that reports from Amnesty International prove that hundreds of thousands of men, women and children are imprisoned, tortured, killed, across the five continents. All this would seem to suggest that an appropriate subject for the section of *Concilium* devoted to moral theology would be: 'Genocide (or homicide) and the right to life'. However, the journal's scientific committee voted in favour of a proposition put forward by the two directors of this section, that an issue should be devoted to 'Suicide and the right to death'. Have we gone mad, or become totally insensitive? Are we still theologians conscious of their duty, Christians conscious of the demands of their faith, human beings with a clear awareness of the present state of the world?

An examination of the last six issues of *Concilium* in the moral theology section proves that it has not been unaware of the problems mentioned above, since five out of the six have direct bearing on some of these problems, or on their economic, social and political context. The subjects dealt with have been: in 1984, 'The Ethics of Liberation—The Liberation of Ethics'; in 1982, 'Unemployment and the Right to Work'; in 1980, 'Christian Ethics and Economics: the North–South conflict'; in 1979, 'The Dignity of the Despised of the Earth'; in 1978, 'The Death Penalty and Torture'. *Concilium* has not, therefore, been oblivious to these problems, and the moral theology section has had the honour of seeing some of its issues very well received in the countries most directly concerned. But our commitment to these problems does not absolve us from considering other important questions, just as the recognition of the importance of hunger and torture does not forbid research into cancer and cardio-vascular diseases, or the examination of other significant mutations in our culture.

ix

The fact is that our experience of death is in the process of changing, our relationship to death is changing. This change is perhaps more noticeable in the countries of the 'First World' than in those of the Second and Third Worlds (not to mention the Fourth), but the causes for it will soon be producing their effects in all parts of the globe. The change has a variety of causes, the most important of which is connected with the progress of medicine, food-hygiene, etc. This has brought about a modification in life expectancy, with the result that, whereas for thousands of years 75 per cent of the population died before they reached the age of 35, and 50 per cent before they reached 15, today in the 'First World' 50 per cent of the population are over 7,5 years of age when they die. Within the next fifty years, the same will be true in the countries of the Third World. Thus death is no longer experienced as an event which cuts off a life at an early stage or in its prime, but rather as a normal and *natural* stage in a life which gets used up and then burns out like a candle. Increasingly, the problem is not so much how to delay death so that life can pass through the proper stages of youth and maturity, but rather whether there are grounds for prolonging our own life, or the life of those we love, beyond a certain point, and so subjecting ourselves or them to more or less devalued, more or less degenerate levels of existence. For if medicine can almost perform miracles, and offer a longer and better life to young people and adults, it can also bring about a situation in which sick people survive in far-from-enviable conditions, and in which old people find themselves subjected to a degraded kind of life. This is an entirely new situation, and one which demands of us theological reflection on the rights human beings may have over their life and their death.

There is another important change, which also affects our understanding of death: in the USA 80 per cent of people die in hospital, and most other countries in the 'First World' will soon have comparable statistics. Death is thus moving into a totally different universe—socially, technically, and from the human point of view. The meaning of death cannot fail to be profoundly affected by this change. A further problem then is: Who becomes responsible for the death of others? On whom is this burden laid? The new circumstances mean that it is doctors and nursing staff who must take responsibility for 80 per cent of deaths, and these are people whose vocation is to heal the sick and lead them back to health. This again is an entirely new situation, demanding reflection on the rights and duties of society in matters of life and death.

These socio-cultural modifications in the meaning of death and its context have repercussions on the very ancient, but, alas, always contemporary, problem of suicide. Important though the psychological factors in suicide may be, it remains true that socio-cultural factors are of decisive significance. Every socio-cultural change in our relationship with death alters the way in which individuals understand their right over their own death, and the right of society to require them to go on living. Suicide is such a complex problem, and raises so many basic and practical moral questions, that it deserves a whole issue of *Concilium* to itself. That, indeed, was our starting-point. But it seemed to us that we could not treat the problem of suicide in isolation from the other problems in our culture which reflect a new experience of death and a change in our relationship to it. That is why the reader will find in the first part of this issue three different sub-sections, which we felt ought not to be kept apart, since each is related, in ways not yet widely recognised, to the other two.

The first sub-section deals with suicide. There is first of all a presentation of the facts: statistics have their uses, as P. Baudry says, and destroy many prejudices and bogus theories. Then follows a sociological approach to the phenomenon of suicide, an approach which has become indispensable since Durkheim. The author we had in mind let us down, and therefore P. Baudry has kindly written this second article also. This is unusual for *Concilium*, but, apart from the fact that it was the result of circumstances, there is no epistemological reason why a sociologist should not deal with both facts and theories. We are grateful to P. Baudry for helping us in this way, and accepting the extra work involved. After a century of psychology and psychoanalysis, there is no need to argue the case for including a psychological approach to suicide (H. Henseler).

A second sub-section deals with the problems raised by the medical and hospital context of death in most Western countries, and before long in many other places. Euthanasia and the urge to preserve life are enormous problem areas, and much has been written about them. We wanted, therefore, to restrict ourselves to a particular aspect. Doctors and those who care for the sick have to exercise a certain right over death and life: how does the exercise of this right modify the traditional understanding of the right of life and the right of death, and also the right *to* life and the right *to* death? We had hoped for two articles: a mainly theoretical treatment (and Lisa Cahill has provided us with one of the best and finest theological articles in this issue), and a more practical one. A nurse who has specialised in ethical reflection on this problem promised us her help, but she withdrew at the last moment, too late for us to find a replacement. That is a considerable loss to this issue. In our Western world, for better or worse, nurses are at the present time involved with the death of 80 per cent of human beings. This means that their experience gives them insights which ought to be reflected on by all. Is it widely known that in a country like the USA, where, technically, professionally and socially, the nursing profession has attained a particularly high level, a serious scientific survey has revealed that 97 per cent of nurses think that the desire of terminally-ill patients to die should be granted, even against the wishes of their families, and that 70 per cent are against the use of very sophisticated procedures for delaying the death of dying patients, 45 per cent of nurses who have taken part in the use of such procedures have done it only to protect themselves against possible legal action, and 25 per cent to avoid conflict with doctors or with the hospital administration. What a pity it is that the voices of these women cannot be heard in this issue. Let us hope that Christian communities, theologians, and the pastoral authorities in the churches, will nevertheless be able to hear them.

The third sub-section is devoted to a claim which has been heard for several decades, but especially over the last ten years in the West, and more recently still in other parts of the world: the right of individuals, not so much to commit suicide, as to have full authority over their own life and death, so that they may die with dignity. Whether or not it approves of this claim, Catholic theology cannot ignore it. Therefore we have invited contributions from people who hold this position, A.-M. Pieper discusses the ethical basis for the claim, and P. Caucanas-Pisier gives a historical survey and details of the thirty or so associations fighting for it in different parts of the world. In doing so, she shows how widespread is the claim, and, especially, underlines the importance of the fact that now, in these movements, the talk is not so much of voluntary euthanasia as of the right to die with dignity. Does this right contradict the right (and the duty) to live with dignity? Here again, Christian theology finds itself faced with a new problem, and it is certainly better that it should be examined and reflected upon than that it should be met with ready-made answers, formulated in a different context and with different problems in view.

It is probably not necessary to go to great lengths to justify the choice of the various themes making up the second part of this issue, which is devoted to theological reflection. Nor do we need to apologise for inviting a contribution from a Protestant theologian. Ecumenism should not be limited to dogmatic theology, even if the differences are often greater and more difficult to resolve in moral theology. (Moralists, it seems, are not admitted to the holy places of ecumenism!) It will be more to the point to emphasise an element which emerges from the juxtaposition of these five articles (or six, if we include with them as we ought, the genuinely theological article by L. Cahill). It will be apparent to the reader that these six articles in no way present a unified, homogeneous doctrine. For example, there is a notable difference between the fairly strict traditional position of N. Banez, and the much more open position of L. Cahill. Similarly, a difference will be observed between N. Banez and D. Power in their interpretation of the increasingly widespread practice of granting religious funeral rites to those who have committed suicide. Nor will the reader be surprised that the reflections of J.-P. Jossua, who maintains his customary stance close to human suffering, sound rather different from the more theoretical considerations of A. Holderegger or H. Kuitert, on the subject of autonomy and liberty. The important theological point to underline seems to us to be elsewhere.

At the present time, as a result of the combination of a variety of factors, many believers, and also many pastoral authorities, wish to reaffirm simple, coherent doctrines, which may lead to clearly-defined patterns of behaviour. From this point of view, this issue may seem a failure. But it is this very failure which seems to us to constitute its success. In the face of problems as new as are most of those discussed in this issue, believing communities may be well-advised, as D. Power says, to act in ways, and to elaborate patterns of conduct, or even ceremonies, which would have been unthinkable fifty years ago. The reaction which, when one is faced with new problems, wants to resolve them without even having posed them, and without having taken the time to observe their various consequences, is a reaction of fear. It betrays a lack of confidence in the power of the Spirit and the faith of believing communities to discover an adequate way of being Christian. We prefer the diversity of points of view represented by the theological articles in this issue. It is vitally necessary that we should fight against the fear which, at one extreme, makes us fall into a rigid traditionalism, or, at the other, into nihilism or irresponsibility. When, as in this present issue, the subject is death, the fear is even greater, since death unleashes in us the most powerful and irrational individual and collective fears. This is all the more reason for making sure that we are not carried away by them. We need strength and magnanimity, in the sense in which Thomas Aquinas used the word, following Aristotle. We also need, we especially need, faith and hope. And charity for all of us, poor mortals who have to face death. We believe that the diversity of the theological points of view expressed here is evidence neither of scepticism nor of intellectual or doctrinal laxism. It is rather the epistemologically necessary condition for the exercise of that faith and that hope, and for a healthy intellectual exercise in theology.

JACQUES POHIER
DIETMAR MIETH

Translated by G. W. S. Knowles

PART I

New Aspects of Various Problems about Death

Patrick Baudry

New and Old Factors in Suicide

FIGURES MIGHT seem of little use in understanding suicides. Any 'totalling' of individual cases might seem of little interest when getting inside the individuals is what is wanted. It might be thought that the general information to be drawn from the statistical data would contribute little to explaining the phenomena. In reality it is important to understand that statistical treatment gives suicide a different character from the one studied by the clinician. The word 'totalling' is incorrect: statistical recording does not produce a brutal juxtaposition of individual tragedies, but throws light on them in different ways. Far from replacing interpretation, numerical analysis initiates it by showing that suicides are not intelligible merely in the light of personal histories, but can also be studied globally. It reveals an important fact: suicide is not just individual, but also social. Suicides are social phenomena.

Correlation of different quantities makes it possible to break with hasty charges and commonplaces; it shows them up for what they are, shows the difference between ideas about suicide and its actual occurrences. For example, what image of suicide lies behind the idea that it is more frequent in autumn and winter than in spring and summer, when the opposite is true? It is easy to see the value of questions of this type—which only statistical treatment is capable of provoking—for an understanding of social attributes to suicide, particularly with a view to prevention.

The reliability of statistical data is sometimes questioned. The figures presented are suspect of inexactitude. It is true that they may be under-estimates, but this fact does not have the importance it is sometimes given. In particular, it does not reduce the value of an analysis of different sub-sets of the data, since the relative proportions are not in question. The attitude of

3

suspicion is not, in fact, serious: it is rooted in prejudice against statistical work, and in the idea that suicide, because of its shameful character, is generally concealed. In practice, however, every suspicious death is the object of rigorous police investigation, against which camouflage is of little effect. The transmission of information to research bodies is a more likely source of weakness in the process of investigation, but this does not mean that rigorous statistical work is impossible. The figures produced, for example, in Czechoslovakia and Hungary—where autopsies on corpses are carried out systematically and camouflage is therefore almost impossible—confirm the social realities of suicide described by studies carried out in countries where investigation of death is less thorough. It therefore requires some obtuseness to question the relevance of such figures.[1]

There is more justification for talk of 'estimates' with regard to attempted suicides. Here there are no national studies, though INSERM (the French national medical research institute) has carried out pilot studies on suicide attempts resulting in hospitalisation, and these have produced solid information. Here again, measuring the phenomena collectively cannot be considered as an introduction to analysis; it is an analysis in itself. Moreover, by revealing constants and regular variations which the individual approach cannot pick up, it encourages new questions.

1. CURRENT DATA

In France suicide is currently in a phase of increase, marked since the 1970s. At the beginning of that decade it was the cause of around 8,000 deaths. In 1980 10,341 suicides were recorded. In 1982 the figure for 'voluntary deaths' was 12,364. Suicidal morbidity (attempts not resulting in death) is variously estimated. INSERM gives a figure of 90,000, with a very high proportion of young people: 28,000 people between the ages of 15 and 24 make suicide attempts.

Moving from suicide to attempted suicide reveals some reversals of proportions. More men that women commit suicide (a ratio of about 3:1), whereas more women than men attempt it. The pilot studies confirm the higher proportion of women: 67 per cent of women and 33 per cent of men.[2] The simplest explanation, though certainly not an exhaustive one, has to do with the nature of the means used. Women use less violent methods than men; they use drugs as poisons much more frequently.

Any attempt at suicide is serious. One would-be suicide in five is seriously or very seriously injured. Forty per cent make further attempts. It is a mistake to talk of 'false suicides'. In the very great majority of cases, suicide attempts are discovered by accident (73.5 per cent), and not as a result of an appeal by the person concerned (26.5 per cent), and discovery takes place in the great majority of cases between one to three hours after the act and three to more than six hours after.[3]

The reversal in regard to sex is repeated in regard to age. Older people commit suicide more, and young people attempt it more. A suicide law can be established: suicide increases with age. The age hierarchy has not changed since 1860. What has changed are the differences between the different age groups; their decline can be observed over the last 20 years. This is the result of two tendencies, the slight reduction in the suicide rate among old people and the great increase, since 1965, in the rate among young people. Since this date there has been a constant increase in the suicide rate among 15–24-year-olds (15 per 100,000 in 1982), and a sharp rise since 1973, particularly marked since 1978 in the 25–34 age group (30 per 100,000 in 1982). These figures are for males. Among women there is no great increase in the suicide rate among the younger groups, and the differences between age groups show a tendency to increase.[4]

Suicide attempts are associated more with young people. They are very frequent among young people between 15 and 24. Sixty-five per cent of attempts are made by people under 35. Does this mean that the intention to kill oneself becomes stronger with age? In our view, such an interpretation is heavily laden with prejudice and should be rejected. We noted above that the sincerity of would-be suicides cannot be doubted. The appeal which is heavily involved in a suicide attempt may have a greater foundation at earlier ages, when a person is more likely to be in touch with others, whereas biological ageing, in our societies, brings with it social death on a large scale. What basis is there for the claim that many suicides are only 'failed attempts' or that the process of making an attempt constitutes a 'lesser' movement towards death? In strictly objective terms, the difference between suicide and attempted suicide lies in the possibility of rescue, which in turn depends on the means used and the degree of isolation of the person.

The masculine preponderance and the over-representation of the old among suicides are common features in almost all countries. The factor of the greater frequency of male suicides is 4 in Norway, 3.9 in Portugal, 3.6 in the USA, 3.4 in Canada, 2.9 in France and Switzerland, 2.5 in Italy and Sweden, and under 2.5 in Japan, Germany, Britain, the Netherlands, Denmark, Belgium and Austria. The factor in the case of older people is 12 in Belgium and France, 11 in the Netherlands, 9.8 in England, 7.7 in Portugal, 7.5 in the USA, 6.4 in Italy, 5.4 in Sweden, and under 5 in other countries.[5]

From reversals of proportion between suicides and attempted suicides connected with sex and age we may now turn to invariances in the socioprofessional affiliation of suicides and suicide-attempters. In 1897 Emil Durkheim wrote, 'Poverty is a protection.' He was wrong. He forgot a sub-proletariat made up of the insane, the unemployed, vagabonds, prostitutes, all sorts of people 'without profession', who in the period when Durkheim was writing, were over-represented in the statistics of suicide rates by professional group.[6] Poverty, economic and social, has never been a protection against suicide, and the social hierarchy of suicides continues today to reflect social inequalities. Just as there is a social inequality in relation to death which, far from diminishing, is becoming sharper,[7] there is a social inequality in relation to suicide. The act of killing oneself is not a luxury reserved to the rich or the prominent, but an expression of the distress of the weak, that is those who have been weakened. Just as Sweden does not have the highest suicide rate, as maintained in the simple view that the Swedes get bored and boredom leads to suicide, nor is it intellectuals who take their lives most. Suicide, which may perhaps be translated as the act of giving oneself wholly over to death, with one's whole body, is far and away most common among the social groups which have an instrumental relationship to the body, labourers and agricultural workers. In the case of attempts, the unemployed, those 'without profession' and invalids are over-represented among both sexes; blue and white collar workers and close to the average, and senior management and the professions are under-represented. These inequalities are sharpened by age. If we compare the suicide rates of the social group least given to suicide (excluding the clergy, among whom it is very rare), we find constantly widening differences. Agricultural workers kill themselves three times as often at age 30–35 as professionals or senior managers, at age 45–50 just under five times as often, and at age 55–60 more than five times as often (figures for 1968–1978).[8]

The relations between suicide and unemployment and between suicide and general crisis are not sufficiently clear to establish general laws. If we were to consider the case of France alone, we would be tempted to propose a simple relationship between the increase in suicides and the increase of unemployment. The USA and West Germany also provide evidence, though less clearly, of this direct relationship. Britain and Italy, however, tell against it. In Britain, where the unemployment rate more than doubled between 1960 and 1979, the suicide rate remained the same at the end of the period as at the beginning. The suicide rate also remained constant in Italy in the period 1970–1978, despite an increase in the unemployment rate of 2.5 per cent[9] The principal effect of unemployment on suicide comes through the family, which the economic crisis may weaken or, on the contrary, reinforce. It becomes clear that economic poverty is not the only factor. For it to result in suicide it has to be combined with isolation. Emile Durkheim's analysis, which showed that the suicide rate varied in inverse proportion to the degree of individuals' integration, is still pertinent. Whether poor or rich, a person commits suicide in a state of isolation.

In the present writer's view, there is a further feature of modern collective life which is significant in this connection. What might be called the absence of signposts, combined with a constant insistence on signs of success, leads to difficulties of adaptation for some people.

2. THE STATE OF ISOLATION

To say that a person takes their life, not 'because they are alone', but 'in a state of isolation', may seem an immense platitude as long as we are inclined to associate suicide too mechanically with abandonment. On the other hand, this assertion can be given weight by reference to statistical data, and it can be shown to be more subtle than it might seem. Suicide becomes more frequent the more the residential community diminishes. In the nineteenth century suicide was an urban phenomenon. Among the likely causes were the uprooting resulting from the flight from the land which broke traditional family ties. In the twentieth century, after a period in which rural and urban rates evened out, suicide has become a rural phenomenon. The suicide rate is lowest for all age groups in Paris, while it is at its highest in rural areas. This fact connects with one previously noted, the disproportionate representation of agricultural workers among suicides. In other words, the statistics tend to indicate that cities do not have, or no longer have, the suicide-generating properties popularly attributed to them.

It is worth while taking this analysis further. It seems reasonable to ask whether cities do not contribute to the shift in the proportions between successful suicides and attempts. One category of arguments in favour of this view is what might be called 'technical'. Barbiturates, which, compared with a rope or rifle, increase the chances of rescue, are more familiar in towns than in the country. Cities are more plentifully supplied with the telephone counselling and other support services which are some of society's provisions for potential suicides. In this connection some writers, such as Baechler and Chesnais, have come to believe that the spread of relief and rescue services may simply increase the number of suicide attempts, on the principle that supply stimulates demand.[10] It is not clear whether suicide mortality and morbidity would be higher in the absence of these telephone services and counselling centres, but it may perhaps be accepted that the fundamental question is whether the professionalisation of such support helps to weaken or discourage local solidarity. Nevertheless another question is also legitimate:

does the presence of a network, whether informal or professional, make it possible for the 'fragmented language' of suicide to be heard at lesser risk than that which leads to a successful suicide? This is not to say that a person who commits suicide would, in a town, decide that a small risk would suffice to gain a hearing. Applied rigorously, this would be to treat would-be suicides as irresponsible, using suicide as just another way of attracting attention. The implication is rather that the differences between suicide and an attempt is perhaps to be found less in the process leading to either than in the state of absolute or relative isolation in which the individuals concerned exist, in the presence or absence of a social context which could influence the choice of methods. Thus, instead of highlighting the danger that supply may provoke demand—though the idea must be kept in mind—this article stresses the preventive value of an urban social context, mass living, of networks of sociability which constitute 'informal interlocutors' who can be activated.

Another comparable factor in this connection is the difference in suicide rates by marital status. Widowers, divorced men and bachelors kill themselves more than married men: five times more, three times more and twice as much respectively. The same differences are found among women, though they are smaller. It is also clear that the presence of children is a determining factor: married people who have children kill themselves less than those who have none. In this connection there has been a remarkable change in one set of statistics. In France before 1972 the daily suicide rate for women was as follows, in descending order: Monday, Tuesday, Wednesday, Friday, Thursday, Saturday, Sunday. After 1972, when the weekly school holiday was moved from Thursday to Wednesday, the order became: Monday, Tuesday, Thursday, Friday, Wednesday, Saturday, Sunday.[11] It seems probable that the reason why women kill themselves less than men is not simply that they choose less 'reliable' techniques, but much more that their roles involve them more than men in networks of solidarity, implant them more deeply in family life and in relationships between generations. This may imply that for women suicide is indeed more part of a strategy of appeal.

The same interpretation may hold for the differences in rates between young people and old. A young person, more than an old person, can situate the act of suicide within a future, and so contemplate 'death as a means', designed to produce change, rather than 'death as an end'. The seasonal character of suicides, the differences in the rates recorded according to the months of the year and the days of the week, also lends itself to this interpretation. There seems to be one firm conclusion to be drawn: suicide has a pattern which is determined by social life. The reason why the seasonal pattern of suicide has changed between the nineteenth century and now, is that it has followed the new social patterns:[12] the spread of holidays, for example, has led to a diminution of suicides in July and August, holiday months when families or age groups come together. We may even go further, emphasising the protective effect of family life and forms of interaction (rates go down at the weekend), and suggest that changing the state of isolation may change the direction of suicide.

3. DIFFICULT TRANSITIONS

The interpretation we are putting forward here on the basis of observational findings corresponds with our existing view of suicide and suicide attempts. There is no space to enlarge on this here, but, briefly, we can say that it situates the act of suicide within a system of interactions. Within this perspective we are interested, not so much in the content of the act, as in the relationship of the person who commits suicide to the people around them.

Various features of the picture can be understood in terms of changes which are difficult to deal with. Examples would be the large increase of suicides among young people, their disproportionate appearance among people who attempt suicide, the high rate of suicide among old people and the effect of family crises (death of a partner, divorce, condemnation to celibacy). One interpretation is that people commit suicide when the change has been forced upon them and they reject it, i.e. it is an escape device. Another explanation is that people kill themselves to change a state of affairs, to speed up a change. Suicides and suicide attempts among young people lend themselves particularly to this interpretation. In relation to poisoning by medication we may note that one adolescent suicide-attempter in three had consulted a doctor in the six months before the attempt, and that in 42 per cent of cases the attempt was made using drugs prescribed for the victim. One may wonder what was not heard or what could not be said at the visit to the doctor, and suggest that the work of prevention, rather than being concentrated exclusively on those who kill themselves (as implied by the reassuring idea that they form a particular class), should be directed to developing listening facilities. The act of killing oneself does not simply indicate a need for love, as can be said too vaguely and sometimes too naively. It is a violent appeal for a redefinition of the inter-relational order.

In the same way an old person's suicide can be understood, not so much as a wish to end it all, as a sort of additional element on top of the social death already suffered. The suicidal behaviour of old people in health institutions is not a proof of their 'regression'; this 'regression' itself should be understood as a tactic designed to modify the inter-relational organisation of hospital life.

Suicide or suicide attempts are disturbing because they provoke feelings of guilt. At a deeper level, perhaps, what is disturbing is the idea that the suicide or the would-be suicide are not in the wrong, the fact that they reveal a social disorder and call for the reconstitution of social ties, a call which goes beyond the capacity of classical prevention.

When a person commits suicide, he or she takes his or her body with them into death. What may seem a truism invites us to examine the meaning of suicide in relation to the social order and networks of social solidarity. It is particularly young people and old people who experience a change in their bodily image. For a long time this change in young people was channelled through a social group and initiation rites, and the elderly body also has been given social significance. It seems likely that the disappearance of these rituals and these meanings does not reduce, but on the contrary, intensifies the deep demand which gave rise to them. The problem is worsened by the way in which today's models define a sort of perfection which can be aimed at only by the 'industrial athlete' who demonstrates his or her success by 'looking good'.

In fact one's relationship to one's body may be indissociable from the 'social body', from a system of rituals which makes it possible for differences to be articulated within a group. The marginalised body, deprived of social involvement in a sexual or emotional exchange, the pathological or suffering body, creates an unbearable state of life; it displays the difficulty of a transition which can no longer be performed within a social framework. Paradoxically—but then suicide is an eminently paradoxical form of behaviour—suicide is killing oneself to win bodily recognition. Suicide is paradoxical and ambivalent—an act to all appearances deadly which may be the intense expression of a will to live.

Translated by Francis McDonagh

Notes

1. J. C. Chesnais *Histoire de la violence* (Paris 1981) p. 189.
2. F. Davidson, A. Philippe 'Epidémiologie du suicide' *La Gazette médicale de France* 90, No 18 (13 May 1983) 1669.
3. See F. Davidson, M. Choquet *Le Suicide et l'adolescent* (Paris 1981) p. 41.
4. See C. Baudelot, R. Establet 'Suicide: l'évolution séculaire d'un fait social' *Economie et statistique* 168 (July–August 1984) 59.
5. See E. Sullerot 'Rapport au Conseil économique et social' *La Démographie de la France* (Paris 1978) p. 63.
6. See J. C. Chesnais, the work cited in note 1, at p. 239.
7. See G. Desplanques 'L'Inégalité social devant la mort' *Economie et statistique* 162 (January 1984) 33ff.
8. See Baudelot and Establet, the work cited in note 4, at p. 62.

9. See J. C. Chesnais, J. Vallin 'Le suicide et la crise économique' *Population et sociétés* 147 (May 1981).

10. See Chesnais, the work cited in note 1, at p. 231; and J. Baechler *Les Suicides* (Paris 1975) p. 557.

11. See F. Aveline, C. Baudelot, M. Beverraggi, S. Lahlou 'Suicide et rythmes sociaux' *Economie et statistique* 168 July–August 1984) 76.

12. See F. Aveline *et al.*, the work cited in note 11, at p. 73.

Patrick Baudry

The Sociological Approach to Suicide, from Durkheim to the Present Day

IT HAS been said that in writing on suicide, Durkheim took an overwhelmingly sociological view of the subject. Of course, we have to recall the particular context and strategy: Durkheim was concerned to have sociology accepted as a taught subject at the university. This cause would be advanced by demonstrating its relevance to a subject which preoccupied the age and which seemed necessarily withdrawn from any overall treatment. We may, therefore, speak of a 'stroke of genius'[1] on the part of the great model of sociology in having chosen a theme which at the time his discipline was deemed incapable of assessing. But we must stress the fact that Durkheim's talent is not entirely rhetorical. While showing the relevance of sociology to the circumstances of an act which seemed essentially a matter of the intimate behaviour and personal history of individuals, Durkheim 'also' wrote well and effectively on suicide. We may also ask what prejudices, in regard not only to sociology but to suicide, were behind such distrust of the social analysis of a form of behaviour which, in fact, most often occurs individually. This may lead us to ask, after Durkheim—eventually pursuing the subject along paths other than those he marked out—what are the benefits of such an analysis.

1. FOR A SOCIOLOGY OF SUICIDE

The idea is still widespread that suicide is a 'mystery'. Yet it is this notion itself which is odd. People seem generally to behave rather as if suicide were inexplicable. Why? The reason is possibly a refusal to confront the matter, and one expressed as a systematic criticism of marginal explanations which never touch on what is 'essential'. Denials of a disturbing reality; a relegation of suicide to the category of mystery in order to escape its scandalous implications. One might also cite a certain type of fatalism which itself deserves detailed examination. Perhaps this tendency also expresses a resistance to the scientific adoption of suicide. Such a resistance should be understood as the sign of a scientifically unacknowledged form of social understanding which typically takes up a stance removed from the ideas of the day. Perhaps what we have here is a reluctance to allow scholars to define and label forms of behaviour which properly concern society as a whole.

But it is a very different thing if any discipline claims that it possesses the monopoly of serious studies on suicide, relegating sociology to the level of a general account of phenomena, which can serve only as an introduction to 'true' analyses. As against such condescension, it is not inappropriate to summarise the Durkheimian heritage.

Suicide (1897)[2] was intended not to categorise the conditions of individual suicides, but to discover the social factors which would allow some understanding of the permanence and variability of suicide rates which result from them. Admittedly the two questions are related, yet they are distinct, and it is important to emphasise this. An interest in the 'collective propensity for suicide' (pp. 33, 336) does not mean that one is 'generalising'.

Any summary runs the risk of a readiness to make quick judgments. Hence a work of four hundred and fifty pages may be contained in a few swiftly evoked formulas, possibly chopped from the original text. 'Every society therefore, at every moment of its history, has a definite inclination to suicide' (p. 10). 'Every society is predisposed to offer a determined number of voluntary deaths' (p. 15). These are striking statements which can have the opposite effect to that intended, and repel instead of attract. We might gain the impression of a society above human beings, deciding their behaviour all the more as they submit to its power. The criticisms may be expressed as social determinism and reductive sociologism. However, Durkheim's expressions, though apparently extreme, are more than slogans. Instead of finding excuses for exaggerations, we must ask whether they are not really major questions (rather than affirmative statements).

Essentially, what (for some people) makes Durkheimian discourse difficult to take is less its pretension to discover the 'major causes' of suicide (as its caricature would wish) and more the fact that it leads to a questioning of all discourse about suicide. If you delimit something, implicitly you require an explanation of what it is trying to find out. It is obvious that sociological discourse itself is not secure from these questions. But we have to state the extent of the thing. That suicide can no longer be attributed to a diabolical nature, mental illness or a psychological inadequacy, and that neurasthenia is no longer any more of an explanation of suicide than heat, the fact of belonging to a certain race, or imitation, may, as negative findings (Part I of the work), seem of little use for any real understanding of the problem. But, apart from the fact that here one is rejecting prejudices (still persistent today), more profoundly we have to understand that it is the individualisation of suicide which is put in question. The fact that impulses, commonly or scientifically cited as causes of suicide, are not the real causes (pp. 144, 147) leads us to look closely at processes of 'explanation' which lead *from individualisation to individuation*, from the study of suicides case by case, from their separate treatment to the hidden location of social processes in the individual, as he or she seems to stand apart from a group as the author of an 'extraordinary' act. Hence, subreptitiously, a social act may be 're-naturalised', no longer in the crude manner of theories of heredity, for instance, but on the basis of the astonishingly simple argument that suicide is the act of an individual. Yet the Durkheimian position on the question tends to a viewpoint different from those which are traditionally cited when considering the act of taking one's own life, whether one is 'successful' or not.

'Let us [as Durkheim recommends] leave aside the individual as individual' (p. 148); that would mean avoiding any repetition of stereotypes, but taking other analyses into account. A finding of major importance should be cited at this point. It seems appropriate to anticipate the development of the Durkheimian approach which I shall engage in later by saying that it is a question no longer of analysing suicide within the framework in which it seems to be set, but, to use a term from the anthropological trend known as 'new communication', to try to reconstruct that framework.[3]

In Part II of his work, Durkheim distinguishes three main types of suicide. Or rather, to avoid all misunderstanding, I should say that these are three social situations, each with its own nuances, apt to provoke acts of suicide in individuals whom their personal history predisposes to allow themselves to be penetrated by outside forces.

The 'egotistical suicide' derives from situations in which an excessive cult of the ego develops. It is explained by the inadequate integration of individuals in their micro-societies. Since the feeling of solidarity is no longer vital enough, and the density and vitality of groups are weakened, an excessive affirmation of the individual ego follows. Egotistical suicide expresses a relaxation of social bonds. The suicide of the melancholic type who planned the circumstances of his death in great detail, who 'analysed himself right to the end' (p. 316); the suicide of the ironic individual who left life apparently indifferent to it: these are forms of this type, in whom one may see the detachment of an individual from the groups to which he or she belongs.

Statistical studies show that suicide varies inversely in relation to the degree of integration of the individual in religious, political and domestic society. It is noteworthy that the family (not only marriage) exerts a protective power.

The 'altruistic suicide' corresponds to situations opposite to those I have just described. Here an excessive degree of integration of the individual is the cause of suicide. The typical case here occurs in the order of duty, and is more often met with in traditional societies. The wife who has to follow her dead husband, the sick old man who has to let himself die, the servants who have to accompany their chief into death are the main situations which may be cited under this head. But there are others belonging to this second type: when the suicide, chosen and no longer obligatory, is seen as an act of virtue, or when it is given a mystic significance. Durkheim saw the army as an environment in our societies apt to the perpetuation of this type.

Durkheim has been criticised for having confused here the act of taking one's own life with that of offering one's own life. Halbwachs has carefully shown the differences between suicide and sacrifice.[4] But perhaps we can see that Durkheim did not 'confuse' anything at all. The act of taking one's own life may indeed take the form of sacrifice. It is this form of expression which Durkheim asks us to consider, while rejecting any radical separation between them which can be established only by subjective feelings and moral considerations. Without putting the two experiences on the same level,[5] without crudely stating that sacrifices are suicides, here, before our eyes, Durkheim initiates a reversal of the main viewpoint: from the stance of the moral qualification of suicides and from that of their understanding. Accordingly, we may ask about the sacrificial dimension of suicide and conduct our inquiry by showing that the persons who have committed or have tried to commit suicide may be the scapegoats of the social group from which they emerge. At the same time we should ask if they are not warning signs of a crisis which concerns the group and demands its participation.

The third type isolated by Durkheim is that of the 'anomic suicide'. It corresponds to disturbances in the equilibrium of the social whole, to instances of deep change where collective existence is upset, and to a state in which needs are not limited and defined (p. 324). The direct successors of Durkheim were able to adopt the concept of anomie, though not with criticism of some of its applications. It has been used especially in American sociology since the 1950s, when *Suicide* was translated into English.[6] But today anomic suicide is still overlooked or merely mentioned in some articles which give an account of Durkheim's study, often reduced to the level of a reflection on social integration.

Nevertheless, beyond its dubious statistical application, I consider that this concept remains of major interest. Durkheim's reflections on it and, prescinding therefrom, on the 'regulation of the passions', allow us to offer a critique of modernity as a system of liberation, in which 'self-realisation' and self-suppression are confused. I shall return to this point. We may also speak of a 'fatalistic suicide'—the fourth type categorised by Durkheim, but which he hardly analysed in full (see p. 311, n. 1)—when the regulation is excessive and when the dominant definition of life makes it intolerably cramped.

2. AFTER DURKHEIM

Two names of French sociologists are often cited: Halbwachs and Baechler. *Les Causes de suicide* is certainly not Halbwachs's best work. He is especially concerned to confirm and correct Durkheim's observations while bringing them up to date. But he hardly develops the sociological theory of suicide. One might go so far as to say that his study, far from being an advance, as achieved by Mauss, is a step backwards. He retains only egotistical suicide, banishes the concept of altruistic suicide, and hardly mentions that of anomic suicide. The criticisms he makes of Durkheim are not always soundly based and some statements are perhaps dubious. But above all, as a whole, Halbwachs's theory is rather platitudinous. Of course I do not wish to say that you should avoid Halbwachs's work: one of his great merits is to have discussed suicide attempts, and he offers information of great importance. But the attribution of suicide to 'type of life' and to the 'complexity of [modern] social life' is imprecise and scarcely convincing. We may feel that Halbwachs is 'sobering' the sociology of suicide by removing its intuitive parts, which are perhaps the best parts of Durkheim's study. Yet, I must aver, perhaps too abruptly, no sober theory can account for a provocative act. Obviously I am not trying to say that anyone can speak of suicide in any terms whatsoever. In fact, it is high time that we scrutinised the way in which we look at it, and ask if the dolorist approach of the victims themselves cannot be replaced. Apart from being imprecise, the theme of the complexity of social life has another disadvantage: it looks far too exclusively at a society destroying itself, at its debilitating social state, instead of showing the virulence of suicide and instead of finding other analytical viewpoints which can develop the process of questioning.

Such an opening is provided by Baechler's work.[7] I shall overlook its deep-seated anti-Durkheimianism which obviously puts the blinkers on it on some occasions. Baechler's merit is to take a comprehensive attitude by referring especially to the writings of Schütz. Baechler seems persuaded that people who commit suicide constitute a category apart. He speaks of a genetic predisposition (p. 91), and says that there is no sociological theory of suicide

(p. 41). All kinds of positions taken are in fact scarcely sociological. Nevertheless, Baechler's suicidology makes a major change. Schütz's distinction between an *Um-zu Motiv* and a *Weil Motiv* (an *in-order-to* motive, and a *because* motive) allows him to understand suicide as a social activity with two possible approaches. We may answer the question 'why?' in terms of 'because'; because we know who the people are who commit suicide and in what circumstances they were brought to take their own lives. But we may also reply in 'in view of' terms, in regard to the *meanings* which the suicides assumed for those who committed them. This second analysis, which is prospective and not retrospective like the first, allows us to understand suicide as a logical step (which does not mean that it is rational), as an answer which an individual finds to resolve a problem. The suicide is no longer subject to investigation as an end, but as a *means*. In this perspective, the suicide is as it were referred to the person who committed it. It is no longer sufficient to say that people take their own lives 'out of' distress, deception, loneliness and so on. It is shown that people also kill themselves *in order to* change a state of things, to arrive at a solution to problems, in various ways which have to be considered.

Another major aspect of Baechler's study, directly related to what I have just described, is his questioning of the traditional assertion that the person who has committed or tries to commit suicide is looking for death. This is an assertion which Baechler rightly qualifies as 'very imprecise' (p. 84). This questioning of a virtual 'finding' does, I think, require more detailed treatment than he gives it, but it is important that here he has hit upon something very decisive. If it is no longer sufficient to say that a person commits suicide because he or she wants to die, then we are no longer concerned merely with the causes of the act but, primarily, with finding out the various meanings it may have. Since the significance of suicide is no longer self-evident, it is necessary to distinguish between different situations, to show and not merely to say that there are various forms of suicide.

Hence suicide ceases to be an absurd act merely explicable in terms of external circumstances. Similarly it loses something of its 'mystery' because it appears as a logical solution. And it is no longer possible to associate it exclusively with depression or with any state of weakness. Suicide (or a suicide attempt) is a positive act and requires an energy which the depressive individual precisely does not possess (see pp. 299, 304). There is room for questioning in one regard here: the suicide happens when the 'desperate' person (as is often said) is getting along much better. Of course that is not to say that people commit suicide 'because' things are getting better. But there is room to take into account a certain power which is connected with the act of self-destruction, and which firmly indicates its *ambivalence*. If we question the idea that suicide means that one wants to die, we move beyond the work of precise typological categorisation which Baechler carried out with such sterling concern. This is tantamount to formulating the hypothesis of a creative perspective, which may seem provocative but is neither 'gratuitous' nor purely theoretical. I shall return to this point.

Baechler distinguishes between four main kinds of suicide which comprise eleven types. There are: escapist suicides (flight, mourning, punishment), aggressive suicides (revenge, blackmail, call for something), oblative suicides (sacrifice, rites of passage), ludic suicides (ordeal, play). They constitute a typology which accounts for actual and attempted suicides. Their 'flexibility' is taken into consideration: that is, their sensitivity to factors intervening in their execution. On this subject, Baechler's main thesis is that the suicidal person is inflexible. This assertion is hardly convincing. It is not only grounded in a questioning of the statistical work which is, in fact, not serious. Above all, it originates in (at the same time as reinforcing) an understanding of suicide which we may describe as individuation. This position may be deceptive. It does not bear out the promise of a 'strategic theory'. Typology is not used for a dynamic understanding of suicide as a social relation.

In the second part of his work, which he devotes to aetiology, Baechler describes an impressive number of facts, reflections and discussions. But from all this he produces no innovative sociological approach. One gets the impression of a systematic prudence which can only find justification within a system of sociologising explanations, which is precisely what has to be examined carefully. Manifestly unconvinced of the relevance of traditional approaches, justifiably rejecting mechanist explanations, Baechler (without any 'change of paradigm'[8] of the necessary fact) does not offer a sociological theory of suicide, and verifies the statement at the beginning of his work that such a thing is impossible. We might think that prudence was advisable when treating a complex and polymorphic problem. But it is perhaps, quite on the contrary, a wager that we have to make: the theoretical risk that must be taken if we are to understand the social dynamics of suicide.

3. A POSSIBLE CHANGE OF FRAMEWORK

Suicides have social causes—that is hardly to be doubted. But, faced with the difficulty of revealing them precisely, without stating truisms (under the cloak of complex language), it might be thought best to leave to the clinical expert the task of understanding the cases with which he or she is faced. But the sociology of suicide cannot be restricted to what one would like to make it in order to show the weakness of its competence. It does not consist only the search for 'causes', as is said. It allows us to describe typical situations, to reveal typical meanings. It does not ask questions only about the object of its research but sets its sights higher too. The reason why Durkheim's approach has been given so much attention here is to free it from ironic or admiring caricatures, but above all because I think that it more than any other seems to pose the question of a sociology of suicide which does not consist in the re-translation into sociological terms of psychological theses. I have said that it asks for a change of framework. Changing the framework does not mean locating the suicide in an enlarged social space, as if to explain from a distance at the risk of losing any contact with unique practices. It means considering suicide as well as possible in a context or 'space' of meanings, and of understanding it so that individual practices should become the objects of alternative approaches.

It is impossible to speak of any one form of violent death without inquiring into the dominant social relations of the death and the violence, without asking what might be the death-bringing effects of a system which 'denies death' (L. V. Thomas[9]), and which administers violence. The social prohibition on living death and violence, on self-construction through their ritualisation[10] gives rise to a confusion of reference-systems. The banishment of social tragedy, the flattening of disruptive conduct, tend (under a veil of tolerance[11] and subversive liberation) to neutralise the irruption of death into life. The modern pacification replaces the symbolic expression of death in relation to life with a quasi-equivalence of vitalism and morbid forms of behaviour, the exploitation of which in sport is paradigmatic of what I am saying. In Black African ritual, the principle of symbolic execution followed by rebirth enabled the necessary integration of death to take place by allowing it to profit from the social dynamism. Today desocialised excess (*excedere*: to emerge from) is brutally taken literally as a will to end it all. Whether one wraps this end in a happy and ecstatic intensity or invests it with the dignity of the last moments of life, with the dignity of a kind of right to die without troubling anyone, it is really always a question of disappearing into the norms of a system which supplies everything, right up to booklets on ways of suicide.

But there is a form of knowledge dominated by death in the midst of life which persists and which reveals precisely, perhaps, the tragic aspect of suicide. Tragedy is never the acceptance of the blank happiness of remaining alive: it relates life to death, it is a 'wisdom of the limits' (Lukács)[12] which circumvents the linear definition of existence.

Therefore it is possible to show that suicides are neutralised precisely because they are vitally related to being as a whole. Suicides remind us of the tension in life and force us to acknowledge it. Durkheim certainly felt this when he wrote of suicides: 'They are only an exaggerated form of conventional practices' (p. 7).

Suicide as an end has to do with the de-medicalisation of death, the re-socialisation of dying, and a new ritualisation of leave-taking. Suicide as a means (which it is in most cases) calls for revived social experience of rupture, and of the reconstruction not only of the individual by means of a crisis of change, but also of the social bond. Loss of self *in* the collective (and not outside it) demands a fundamental solidarity. In this perspective one can only protest against new prevention measures which certain hospital departments have begun to introduce.

Translated by J. G. Cumming

Notes

1. J. Duvignaud *Introduction à la sociologie* (Paris 1966) p. 90.
2. First French edition, *Le Suicide* (Paris 1897). English translation, *Suicide*, London, 1952. References here are to the Paris edition of 1981, in order to preserve the present author's interpretation. (*Tr.*).
3. See, e.g., P. Watzlawick, J. Weakland and R. Fish *Changements, paradoxes et psychothérapies* (Paris 1975) p. 116.
4. See *Les Causes du suicide* (Paris 1930) pp. 479, 480.
5. See *De la Division du travail social* (Paris 1978) p. 226.
6. See P. Besnard 'Le Destin de l'anomie dans la sociologie du suicide' in *Rev. Franc. Sociol.* (1983) 605–629.
7. *Les Suicides* (Paris 1975).
8. See T. Kuhn *The Structure of Scientific Revolutions* (Chicago 1962).
9. See *Anthropologie de la mort* (Paris 1975); *Mort et pouvoir* (Paris 1978).
10. P. Baudry *Mort, violence et sacré dans la société moderne* (Paris 1983).
11. See M. Horkheimer *Eclipse of Reason* (London 1947) p. 31.
12. See G. Lukács *Soul and Form* (London 1971) p. 269.

Heinz Henseler

The Psychology of Suicide

1. THE HISTORICAL SITUATION

UNTIL ABOUT a hundred years ago the inquiry concerning the motives underlying a man's decision to take his own life was almost entirely left to theologians, philosophers and jurists. Very simple and conscious motivation was taken for granted, and the moral responsibility of the suicide for his action was not in doubt.

It is to a sociologist (E. Durkheim, 1897) that we owe the original suggestion that the freedom of suicide may be in question. He gave empirical evidence that suicides are more prevalent when social conditions are unfavourable. Eight years later, a psychiatrist (R. Gaupp, 1895) drew attention to 'personality factors of an abnormal kind' in suicides, and pointed out the need for careful distinction between motives determined by particular situations and pathological causes.

Now there was a danger that in a psychiatry predominantly orientated by biological concepts the interpretation of suicide would go to the opposite extreme. The act of suicide was regarded as a symptom or complication of a 'depression' usually of an 'endogenous' or 'psychopathic' origin, and consequently as the expression of an inescapable illness or development, in comparison with which the motives triggering off the suicides, and their therapeutic consideration could be regarded as of little importance. However, the discovery of unconscious motives and the possibility of their disclosure through analysis (S. Freud, 1916) made it possible, while not doubting the existence of constitutional factors in the rise of suicidal impulses, to leave considerable room for an unconscious psychical dynamism. This saved those

21

in danger of suicide both from premature moralistic condemnation and also from the resignation of the therapists.

Does this mean that the act of suicide is from the start to be regarded as a pathological act, as the 'conclusion of a pathological development' (Ringel, 1953), and consequently irrational and not responsible? This question forgets that medicine was long ago forced to abstain from drawing clear boundaries between health and sickness, and that even in the case of a predominantly psychical problem we must discover in the individual case what are the biological, and/or sociological, or social and psychological conditions of an act of suicide, and how in it, conscious motives, for which the agent is responsible, are mixed with unconscious ones, for which he is not. To make a decision here, we do not need merely to listen carefully, but also to have theoretical knowledge about the biological, sociological, and depth-psychological context.

In the following study we shall describe under the title of 'the psychology of suicide', the ideal-typical dynamic of the psychic factors and powers which, allowing also for possible biological or sociological disabilities, are of decisive importance in the origination of serious suicidal intentions, suicidal impulses, and attempted or actual suicides. This ideal-typical dynamic, according to psychiatric classification, applies to persons suffering from a neurotic disturbance. It is these who form the great majority—over 90 per cent—of suicides. More unusual suicidal actions, such as those arising from bankruptcy, from ritual, political or psychotic grounds, cannot here be considered. No distinction is made between the degrees of seriousness of the suicidal impulses or acts. There is good empirical proof for the claim that the simple, clear, suicidal impulse is just as rare and extreme a variant as the purely demonstrative attempted suicide. Between these extremes are found the majority of those whose lives are at risk through suicide, with all sorts of combinations and mixtures of motives tending to destroy and to preserve life, (appeal, revenge and the desire to retaliate).

2. AN EXAMPLE

A schoolboy from a Senior Secondary School aged 17 attempted suicide with 30 tablets of Valium and a half-bottle of wine. He reported that for two years he had been entertaining the thought of suicide. Now he had determined to put it into action. Three days previously his girl friend had missed her period, and both of them, with daily mounting anxiety, had feared a pregnancy. On the third day, in a mood of depression and irritation they had gone for a long walk. This morose mood lasted till evening. Even on parting, they had quarrelled. He went home in dejection. He spent the evening smoking in his room, until at one o'clock he decided to go into the forest and poison himself.

What had led to this act? Even before I could speak to the young man, I heard many conjectures. His mother rang me up in tears. She complained that in the last year or two he had become so strange, had developed such strange philosophical views, according to which life was not worth living, and one had really a duty to make an end of oneself. He played truant from school, wandered around at night, and smoked hashish. Formerly he had been so religious. His minister interpreted his attempted suicide as the consequence of a loss of faith. His father's attempts at discipline were ineffectual. Could I help?

The doctor made reference to the young man's weak physical build, and was of the opinion that a mere glance could confirm that his character was lacking in strength. She proposed to treat him with tonic preparations and counselling help. The social worker to whom the patient for the first time mentioned the fears of pregnancy, urgently advised a consultation with a view to a legal abortion. Thus there was a variety of explanations of the circumstances or motives of the attempted suicide. These explanations were the more confusing because none of these interpretations is to be rejected out of hand. Faced by such explanations today, people are inclined to adopt the fashionable formula, that suicidal acts are of 'multi-factorial origin', and that, consequently, help of different kinds is to be given. What makes this formula so questionable is (i) that the motives or circumstances are of very different importance, and (ii) that it is not at all clear whether all the factors are already known, and because (iii) very sensitive people do not respond as a rule to therapeutic activism. More useful is the search for the decisive motive, whose removal, it is to be expected, will lead to a considerable alleviation of the suicidal tendency.

Now, to all appearance, the fear of a pregnancy in the girl friend was the decisive motive. That this was not the case was shown by the patient's reaction to the news that in the interval menstruation had begun. He was indeed relieved, but still remained convinced that his life was not worth living. His attempted suicide had indeed not succeeded, but he would repeat it at the next opportunity.

One of the difficulties in finding the psychodynamically decisive factors among the many possible circumstances and motives is that motives can only be inferred from the subjective experience of the person concerned. Not only this, it is further true that, as a rule, he is not conscious or not fully conscious of them. It is consequently important not only to listen carefully to the person in danger of suicide, but also to watch where there are indications that the patient is concealing, or would like to conceal, something from himself. Thus the patient in this case had spoken of the friction which dominated the encounter between him and his girl friend on the last day, and also mentioned that he had parted from her in anger. The rather casual mention of this fact had remained in my memory. So I asked what had been the cause of the quarrel. The patient hesitated very much in answering. It was evident that he wished to hold back something, or even to hide its importance from himself. When I conveyed this impression to him, he was able, after some hesitation, to tell me that at the moment of parting she had shown tenderness to him. She indicated that she would like to sleep with him, an experience which, in the situation, she had found comforting. The patient felt himself unable to comply, and told her so. Disappointed by his rejection, his girl friend became very angry, and reproached him—it was always she who had to make the advances, what sort of a man was he?

The patient felt deeply wounded, the more so that the reproach was true. After parting he attempted to get over the injury, and to play down to himself its significance. Some hours later he decided to attempt suicide, with the conscious reflection that now at last he would overcome his cowardice, and put his long-entertained suicidal thoughts into action.

To express it more theoretically, the patient had in part again repressed or denied the insult, and in part cancelled it out by a counter-reaction, by deciding upon a 'manly' action. It was only my intervention that made him become fully conscious of the insult again and its real significance for his decision to commit suicide, and thus accessible to treatment. The treatment consisted of discussing in a number of sessions the background causes of his vulnerability, his narcissistic problem. This took the form, as it happened, of painful doubts of his virility, in relation to the fact that he 'still' masturbated. He had, as a result of reading church publications, accepted the theory that through masturbation he was losing essential protein, and thereby weakening his power to love and his virility. In the reproaches of his girl friend he saw the proof and the feared discovery of his weakness.

The very possibility of talking with somebody about the insulting remark of his girl friend and his fears in relation to masturbation, gave visible relief to the patient, a relief to which he gave intelligible expression. The further and decisive release consisted of his being able to bring into the foreground and to question his fundamental narcissistic problem, i.e. his long-continued but painfully repressed doubts as to his virility. These had, of course, only a superficial connection with his masturbation. This meant that attention had been shifted from the superficial cause to a largely unconscious inner problem which was associated with it. This shift at the same time removed the acute danger of suicide. The patient was now able to consider with me what had led to such doubts about himself, and whether the grounds for them were valid. It is not necessary to enter into further details in this context.

3. GENERAL RULES

The purpose of this case-history is to demonstrate, by means of an example, a possible course of exploration in the case of an attempted suicide, in which the question is raised concerning the decisive motives, and becomes the central problem. The search for the motive is, however, made difficult:

(a) by widespread prejudices concerning the background of attempted suicide (Henseler, 1971);

(b) by premature declarations that external problems are the cause, (e.g. unexpected pregnancies, bad conscience, money difficulties, bad social conditions, etc.), the significance of which is undeniable, but whose importance for the discharge of the suicidal impulse can only be explained by reference to the subjective outlook of the person in question;

(c) by the distortion of the conscious experience of the patient by repressive activities that thrust down essential areas of motivation into the unconscious.

Thus, if general conjectures, external strains, and even the conscious reports of the suicidal person about his motivation, provide only inadequate indications, we might be in despair, if there were not rules which have proved themselves useful. One such rule tells us that suicidal crises are not brought about by unspecific psychological strains, but only by such as are experienced as insulting. We have therefore to ask, what has so insulted the patient that he believed that he could no longer continue to live.

Further, we are helped by the circumstance that if intolerable insults lead at all to suicidal acts, then it is only for a short period. To put it otherwise, this means that the triggering insult is to be looked for minutes or hours, rarely a few days before the suicidal act. (Where there have been thoughts of suicide of long standing, there is always also a final impulse). The impulse regarded as insulting nearly always proves to have a specific content, in the sense that it resembles an allergen that sets off a latent allergy; this means that the insult stands in a close relation of content to a latent narcissistic fundamental problem. If this has been discovered, the danger of suicide is often quickly reduced. This is achieved by the patient being made aware that the triggering insult is only a new link in the old chain of problems; while, on the other hand, the patient and the counsellor have been given the possibility of looking into the narcissistic fundamental problem, which nearly always proves to have an inadequate basis or none.

4. THE PSYCHOANALYTIC UNDERSTANDING OF SUICIDAL ACTION

The concepts introduced in the case-history and in the statement of general rules, relating to the narcissistic insult and the fundamental narcissistic problem, must in conclusion be placed in the context of psychoanalytic theory from which they derive.

The pre-scientific understanding of suicide already etymologically implies a theory, namely the turning of aggression against one's own person. From this a premature inference has been drawn, that the potential suicidal person suffers from an inability to deal adequately with aggression and that therapy must consist in taking aggression seriously, and channelling it into discourse (Pohlmeier, 1978).

This assumption overlooks Freud's discovery (1918), that aggression is directed against the self when the relation to a disappointing object, which is nevertheless experienced as indispensable, is threatened. What is at stake is therefore not simply a conflict of aggression, but the rescue of an object-relation. Rage must be directed against the self, in order that it may not destroy the relation.

It might be objected that suicide destroys the relationship any way. However, for the psychical experience of the typical suicide, the act of suicide is indeed consciously an act of self-slaughter, but unconsciously a flight into a condition of rest, of comfort, of freedom from tension, harmony, ecstasy, and indeed triumph. Expressed in more theoretic terms, a regression into the earlier forms of relation, of harmonious fusion with the primary object. Suicidal patients regularly make a distinction between dying and killing oneself.

The goal of rescuing an object-relation by the act of suicide raises the question as to why this object is so indispensable. Freud answers this in 1915 by saying that the object clearly has narcissistic quality. This means that the object is valued not so much as an independent individual but rather as a substitute for one's own actual or imagined shortcomings. If it disappoints in this function, or is even totally lost, the awareness of these defects becomes overpowering and intolerable. Put in another way, the subject regulates its labile narcissistic system partly with the help of an object loved in a narcissistic manner (Freud, 1914), which is also called a self-object (Kohut, 1973). The author described in 1974 and 1978 how we can picture to ourselves the way in which a labile narcissistic regulatory system comes into being and with which preferred mechanisms it operates in such a process in order to compensate for disturbances. The most important of these are a negative attitude to reality which is actually, or is thought to be, injurious, and an idealising misrepresentation of it. This applies also to one's own person and objects. The failure of a narcissistic object to fulfil its function is experienced as an insult. If this insult is so severe that it can no longer be neutralised by its denial and idealisation, an attempt is made to compensate by the activation of a fantasy of the individual having the task of fusing in a harmonious unity with a diffusely experienced archaic object. In 1974 the author tested and confirmed these hypotheses in relation to 50 patients picked at random, subsequent to suicide attempts. Various later investigations by other scientists confirm the relevance of this concept (see also Henseler and Reimer, 1981).

5. CONSEQUENCES FOR THE TREATMENT OF PERSONS IN DANGER OF SUICIDE

The theoretic interpretation of the psychodynamics of suicidal persons which I have just described, has decisive consequences for the way they need to be treated. In nearly all cases of persons in danger of committing suicide, the assumption of a narcissistic crisis leads speedily to an understanding of the actual situation and to a fruitful therapeutic approach.

In order to give a rough orientation it has proved useful to look for inferiority feelings in the three following areas: doubts relating to one's own virility or femininity, doubts relating to powers and ability, and doubts relating to acceptability in general. In order to recognise the type of inferiority and to make the person concerned aware of their full subjective content and significance, we ought to take account of what he tells us about himself, the account given of him by 'significant others', but most of all, his interaction with the person counselling him and dealing with him.

His account of himself, consciously and superficially marked by ideas of inferiority, neutralises the doubts of his own value by means of secret or unconscious fantasies of greatness. The narcissistic problem is as a rule attached to a partner, from whom the actual conflict originates. If one attends to the description of the suicidal person's relation to him, one gains important insights relating to the narcissistic function of this person, and consequently relating to the patient's problem. Disappointment caused by the partner in the conflict leads as a rule to the suicidal person looking around quickly for a substitute. The counsellor offers himself in this role (assuming that he comes on the scene in time). If he at first is patient, and permits the situation to be structured by the suicidal person, he can experience here and now the problem of the patient in the interaction that now develops. This has the incomparable advantage that one can work at it with him in an equally concrete manner. If the narcissistic reaction is accepted by the counsellor, he can reflect upon it together with the patient, especially in dealing with its origin. If one can show the suicidal person, in the here and now of the interaction, what his aim is, in trying to use the counsellor and other persons in his environment—i.e., what doubts he is trying thus to allay, one can relativise the patient's anxious fixation upon his actual situation, and apply oneself to the question of discovering what his fundamental narcissistic problem is, what is its origin, and how valid it actually proves to be when dispassionately considered.

Translated by David Cairns

Litnerature

Durkheim, E. *Le Suicide* (Paris 1960 E.T. *Suicide; a study in sociology* Glencoe, Ill. 1951; London 1972).

Freud, S. *Zur Einführung des Narzissmus* (1914) Collected Works X (London 1946) pp. 137–170.

Freud, S. *Trauer und Melancholie* (1916) Collected Works X (London 1946) pp. 427–446.

Gaupp, R. *Ueber den Selbstmord* (Munich 1905).

Henseler, H. 'Selbstmord und Selbsmordversuch—Vorurteile und Tatsachen'. *Deutsches Aerzteblaft* 68 (1971) 789–791 and 2892-2894.

Henseler, H. *Narzisstische Krisen. Zur Psychodynamik des Selbstmords* (Reinbeck 1954; 2^0 Wiesbaden 1984).

Henseler, H. 'Die Theorie des Narzissmus' in *Die Psychologie des 20. Jahrhunderts* (Zurich 1976) III at pp. 459–477.

Henseler, H. and Reimer, Ch. *Selbstmordgefährdung—Zur Psychodynamik und Psychotherapie* (Stuttgart 1981).

Kohut, H. *The Analysis of the Self* (London 1971).

Pohlmeier, H. *Selbstmord und Selbstmordverhütung* (Munich, Vienna, Baltimore 1978).

Ringel, E. *Der Selbstmord; Abschluss einer krankhaften Entwicklung* (Vienna and Dusseldorf 1953).

Lisa Sowle Cahill

Respecting Life and Causing Death in the Medical Context

IN THE context of medical practice, the distinction between those means of life support which are 'ordinary' and those which are 'extraordinary' captures both the Christian commitment to the value of life, and the Christian recognition that that value is limited, not absolute. To honour and protect the value of human life, especially of innocent life, Christianity has forbidden direct killing to end a painful existence. In the medical context, such killing is referred to as euthanasia or 'mercy-killing'. However, recognising the importance of *quality* of life for the enhancement of human dignity, theologians and teachers have not seen biological life as an end in itself. Traditional Catholic teaching about care of the sick and suffering considers the appropriateness of death, even as it affirms the goodness of life; it recognises that although suffering can be integrated into the mystery of Christ's death and resurrection, it also can be futile and destructive. Efforts to support physical life can with moral legitimacy cease when continued biological existence becomes an occasion of deterioration rather than of development of personal spiritual and moral integration.

In an important address, Pope Pius XII expresses the *flexibility* of the Catholic view of medical care for the seriously ill or dying. He observes that both 'natural reason and Christian morals' ground the right and the duty in case of serious illness to take the necessary treatment for the preservation of life and health. Nonetheless,

normally one is held to use only ordinary means—according to circumstances of persons, places, times, and culture—that is to say, means that do not involve any grave burden for oneself or another. A more strict obligation would be too burdensome for most men and would render the

29

attainment of the higher, more important good too difficult. Life, health, all temporal activities are in fact subordinated to spiritual ends.[1]

This statement can serve as a concise point of departure for our discussion, since it will allow us, without recapitulating in detail the whole Catholic medical-moral tradition, to raise three questions about euthanasia and the provision of means of life support. First, what is the substance of the position representatively expressed by Pius XII? Second, what are the elements of change and continuity in present expressions of this teaching in comparison to its formulation almost thirty years ago? Third, what are the key points of the teaching about which questions currently are raised, and in regard to which revisions sometimes are recommended?

In brief overview, it can be said, first, that the heart of the teaching is that, while direct killing of the sick is excluded, the omission of life-sustaining measures is permitted if they prove either futile or oppressive. It is assumed that the patient or a delegated proxy acting in his or her best interests will be the primary decision-maker. Second, while direct euthanasia continues to be excluded and the omission of extraordinary means permitted, certain emphases have shifted. Rather than rushing to repudiate in no uncertain terms the moral reprehensibility of killing the innocent, and to endorse the sanctifying potential of suffering, current statements begin by considering as a whole all aspects of the good of the person, and admit more directly that prolonged or acute suffering often has extremely negative consequences for that good. Third, the questions which motivate reconsideration of the substance of the teaching are whether it is ethically meaningful to insist upon the distinction between acts of commission and omission (that is, active and passive or direct and indirect killing); and whether there are any means of life support which are *always* 'ordinary', that is, indispensable from the standpoint of Christian ethics, no matter what the condition of the patient.

1. LIFE: RESPECT AND CARE

Richard A. McCormick, SJ, has offered some insights into the significance of Pius XII's statement which are both illuminating and provocative. In an essay commenting on treatment decisions for critically impaired newborns, McCormick uses the vastly increased capability of medicine to sustain such infants as an occasion to pursue the core of the traditional definition of an 'extraordinary' means.[2] The very proliferation of modern medical resources has resulted in confusion about whether these resources should always be employed, and if not, then what criteria should determine their use and who should decide whether the criteria apply. It may happen in practice that physicians bring all available skills and remedies to bear on a case before adequately considering the likelihood of significant, long-term benefit to the infant. Or, on the other side, parents still shocked and grieving at the lot of their child refuse consent for all treatment if no treatment holds out for them and the infant the hope of a 'normal' life. McCormick presses the point that it is vital to ask for a nuanced estimate of the quality of the life sustained, and that such inquiry is not at all new to the tradition. Physical life has never been defined as an 'absolute' in the Christian tradition, that is, something to be preserved at all costs. As a physical good, it is subordinate to spiritual goods, and is important precisely because it is the necessary condition of their enjoyment. It ought, however, never to supplant them. Thus we consider the criterion of 'burdensomeness' in determining when life should be yielded up to the inevitability of death.

But, asks McCormick, what *are* the spiritual ends and the higher good which Piux XII mentions? Further, what is it about extraordinary means that makes them burdensome and thus optional? He responds that the most important good of life in the Judaeo-Christian tradition is love of God, and that this good is fulfilled through love of neighbour (1 John 4:20–21). Physical life is good for an individual, then, to the extent that it permits the development of 'human *relationships*, and the qualities of justice, respect, concern, compassion, and support that surround them'.[3] In traditional treatises and moral manuals, this insight was expressed negatively in terms of the 'hardship', or 'inconvenience' which an extraordinary means presented to the patient, and included the grave disruption to meaningful relationships caused by excruciating pain, financial decimation, or uprooting geographical relocation.[4] McCormick observes that in the cases of some infants (and adults) the potential for relationships is prohibited by the physical condition itself. Examples that he gives are severe mental retardation which eliminates any capacity for experiencing the relations of love for which life is destined, and physical disability so consuming that life becomes a 'mere effort for survival'.[5] McCormick's analysis makes clear that the distinction between ordinary and extraordinary means has always required a quality of life assessment, one which permits sensitivity to and is relative to the circumstances of the individual. He concludes by insisting that it is not a question of whether the person who is permitted to die is valuable, but whether continued physical life is a value for him or her, and that a decision must be made in terms of his or her good alone.

To summarise, the 'ordinary' means is one which supports life in a condition permitting as life's central project the development of personal relationships. The extraordinary means is one which is excessively painful or inconvenient, that is 'burdensome', hence interfering radically with a genuinely human direction and focus of life. Although at different historical stages of the development of the definitions, different examples of ordinary and extraordinary means have been proposed, it has always been acknowledged that they will vary with the physical condition and personal strengths of the patient, as well as with the levels of availability and effectiveness of various medical treatments. For instance, in the seventeenth century, the Spanish Cardinal, John de Lugo, did not consider it necessary to use any 'artificial' means to support life, whereas today some of the most readily available and efficacious remedies are laboratory-produced pharmaceuticals. The one moral limit which has not been considered relative to circumstances is the prohibition of direct killing. Euthanasia is characterised by Second Vatican Council as 'opposed to life itself', as an act which will 'poison human society', and which is 'a supreme dishonour to the Creator'.[6]

2. THE PERSPECTIVE: SHIFTS AND BALANCES

Despite continuity in the substance of Catholic teaching on care for the sick and dying, there have been some notable shifts in approaches to the problem. If one reads earlier and later magisterial documents or theological manuals, one encounters differences in the way the good of the person is construed, suffering interpreted, and moral norms proposed. Taken together, these amount to a significant change in the manner the ethics of care for the dying is understood. The opening paragraphs of the recent *Declaration on Euthanasia* (1984) serve as an indicator. Before citing them, a context of interpretation may be established by recalling the words with which a noted American moral theologian introduced in 1957 his consideration of 'the euthanasia movement':

> this movement is imbued with the same principles, the same lack of appreciation of the meaning and value of human life, that characterized the 'philosophy' of the totalitarian State and that resulted in the horrible mass murders of so-called useless persons.[7]

Undoubtedly, it is of no small significance that the Nazi atrocities are for the author cited a memory of the recent past, one which we might do well not to allow to fade. Nonetheless, the authors of the 1984 *Declaration* more successfully further dialogue by recognising conscientious conviction on both sides. They admit that euthanasia is usually proposed out of concern for the patient, not a desire to dispose of him or her. As the *Declaration* states, people of modern society 'experience no little anxiety about the meaning of advanced old age and death' and 'also begin to wonder whether they have the right to obtain for themselves or their fellowmen an "easy death", which would shorten suffering and which seems to them more in harmony with human dignity'.[8] Furthermore, the pleas of the ill for their own deaths are to be understood as 'a case of an anguished plea for help and love'.[9] The focus of discussion has shifted from condemnation of immoral acts to exhortations to understanding and a sincere commitment to provide care sufficient to make demands for death unnecessary. From the 'inviolability' of 'innocent life' considered more or less as an abstract category, attention has moved to the plight of the concrete individual, and to the totality of elements which make up his or her welfare.

Suffering and its meaning have always played a prominent part in Catholic discussions of sickness and death. Again, however, a shift has occurred, most importantly at the level of the duty to *relieve* suffering. The *Declaration on Euthanasia* observes that pain 'often exceeds its own biological usefulness and so can become so severe as to cause the desire to remove it at any cost'.[10] While it calls suffering 'a sharing in Christ's passion', it recommends the use of painkillers for 'the majority of sick people', even if these medicines reduce consciousness and diminish resistance to death.[11] While Pope Pius XII approved the use of such analgesics, his tone was somewhat more reserved.[12]

The apostolic letter of John Paul II, 'On Human Suffering', sheds additional light on current views of 'extraordinariness' in supporting life. The theme of the letter is the salvific meaning of suffering, but the paradigm of suffering is the Good Samaritan (Luke 10:29–32). It is an active rather than a passive suffering, a suffering for the sake of the kingdom which actively tries to alleviate the suffering of others. Thus the burden of redemptive suffering is shifted from the sick and dying to those who attend them. Occasionally care-givers may relieve pain by omitting the measures which prolong pain as well as life. The omission of extraordinary means may now be seen as an active duty of love, rather than as a borderline 'permission' just this side of the limit separating the forbidden. Repeating the criterion of burdensomeness, the *Declaration* acknowledges that 'the use of therapeutic means can sometimes pose problems', and affirms the popular phrase 'a right to die' as 'the right to die peacefully with human and Christian dignity'.[13]

3. A 'RIGHT' TO DIE?

One somewhat problematic element in recent views of death and dying is the tendency to phrase the claim of the patient in terms of a 'right to die'. This usually refers to the withholding or removal of extraordinary means, but it can also indicate a claim for active support in seeking death, extending to 'acts of commission'. Aside from the issue of the morality of active euthanasia, there are two reasons why it appears strange to speak of death as a 'right'. The first is that we usually perceive *life* as a fundamental good (to which we have a 'right') and death as a deprivation of it. The second is that, if the rights of persons correlate with the duties of others to support those rights, then a right to die entails a duty to kill, or at least to precipitate death by some indirect means. At the same time, we generally understand one of our primary duties to others (especially the incapacitated or incompetent) to be to protect and serve their lives. The obvious answer to these objections is that death is not a good 'in itself', as life is, but a circumstantial one. Life is a value whose appeal is immediate and whose claim on moral choice is presupposed. But death is a good only for those individuals for whom physical life is irreversibly deprived of the potential for meaningful human relationships at even a minimal level. Further, it can be maintained that even in the face of a right to die, the prohibition against direct killing of the innocent still holds.

Even with these qualifications, however, the idea of a 'right to die' remains problematic. This is because it tends to cast the notions of life, death, suffering, and mutual human support in *individualistic* terms. On this point Western cultures can be contrasted to many non-Western ones, which is no doubt why social movements in favour of euthanasia and suicide are predominantly Western phenomena. Most Western societies tend to focus on the individual person in defining moral claims and obligations. It is thought to be of paramount importance to preserve the autonomy, the freedom, and the dignity of each individual, and ethics begins with definitions of these goods. In such a perspective there is almost no notion of meaningful suffering, and loss of independence looms as a fearsome evil. In many non-Western cultures, the community or society and the family are the points of departure for moral thinking. In these more communitarian perspectives, loss of individual capacity and dependence on others may not present themselves as radical violations of a 'worthwhile' human life. While these non-Western cultures will not necessarily preserve the life of every declining individual at all costs, they are more able to place the past and present significance of that life in a larger network of relations and goods, both personal and social. It may be more readily assumed that the family or community will care for its weaker members (especially the elderly), and that to accept such care is not a degradation. Birth, life, and death fit into a larger pattern, in which prominence belongs to the general rhythm of the life of the community, rather than to the individuality of its members. While it is true that in a society in which the good of the whole is paramount, there may be insufficient appreciation of the value of some individual members, more relational interpretations of membership in community may bring to Western eyes a renewed vision of humanity's intrinsic sociality.

On this point it will be helpful to recall that the Western Catholic tradition of medical morality has inclined toward act-centred and individualistic analyses of moral obligation. A fruitful counterpoint is to be found in the Catholic tradition of *social ethics*, as embodied for instance in the modern papal social encyclicals. In the Church's social teaching, personal dignity is always elaborated and protected within a context of the common good. In this context, natural sociality and interdependence are affirmed, and 'rights' are never proclaimed without due attention to duties. Duties which must correlate with any right are the duty to respect the rights of others and the duty to use well and in the service of God and other persons the goods to which we lay claim with 'rights' language. To bring the concept of common good back to the question of 'right to die', we may say that the primary *duty* of the person is love of God and neighbour. A person may legitimately claim a right to die only if continued life detracts from fulfilment of that duty, and if the active appropriation of death can be understood as an act of obedience to God and of charity to others. Furthermore, it is the duty of those surrounding the patient to model their care on the Good Samaritan, willing to sacrifice so that those near death may be comforted, and their days made worthwhile. In this way, the desire for death may be avoided.

4. QUESTIONS: DIRECT AND INDIRECT KILLING

It remains to pose a few questions regarding the two key distinctions underlying the Catholic teaching about causing death in a medical setting. These two are the differentiation of the 'ordinary' (mandatory) from the 'extraordinary' (optional) treatment and the moral separation of acts of omission from those of commission. Throughout the history of its development, the distinction of ordinary and extraordinary means has been refined and nuanced, so that means which were once unusual, burdensome, and probably useless, such as most types of surgery, are now considered medically useful and capable of significant contribution to quality of life.[14] In recent decades, however, another shade of meaning has coloured the term 'ordinary means'. The new meaning is usefulness in light of the *total* physical condition of the patient.

The relevant question is whether a means which prolongs life by successfully meeting an immediate, basic physical need may be omitted as 'extraordinary' if the person is suffering from a condition unrelated to the basic need, but which will gravely affect quality of life, and perhaps also life expectancy. An older example is the case of the diabetic who has terminal cancer, and who is dependent on insulin. May the insulin be omitted in view of the prognosis regarding cancer, even though insulin and cancer are unrelated, or related only in so far as they affect the same person?[15] A newer and presently more realistic example is the case of the irreversibly comatose patient who is dependent on intravenous feeding for life support. Does even such a basic form of care as nutrition become extraordinary in cases where 'quality of life' is virtually non-existent?[16] Although reluctance to cease provision for essential human needs is understandable and appropriate, it is equally appropriate to view the patient as a whole, rather than as an amalgam of separate parts and functions. Thus, if discontinuance of *all* types of life support measure is in the best interests of the patient, such a course of action does appear to be justified. The only remaining and important issue is whether in a particular case, all other avenues of enhancing the living and dying of the person have been explored.

The final question to be raised is both controversial and perplexing. While many see any contemplation of direct killing of patients as an assault on the dignity and safety of all innocent persons, others conscientiously believe that since life under some conditions can be a fate more deplorable than death, 'care' can sometimes take the form of active killing. Those who offer this argument are unconvinced by the rejoinder that there is not only a factual difference but a moral chasm between acts which 'permit' death by not resisting it, and those which 'cause' death by directly ending life. One of the most difficult tasks in the debate about euthanasia is to define with precision the moral difference between omission and commission. First of all, both ways of bringing death about involve moral *decisions* followed by overt physical *actions*, e.g., turning off a respirator, removing an IV tube, or just checking out of a hospital. Second, causing death by omission can be morally reprehensible given circumstances in which a worthwhile life could be saved or prolonged. Perhaps one of the strongest reasons against the justification of direct, active killing is that to do so is to institute a *practice* which could be extended to innocent individuals in less drastic circumstances than the suffering and perhaps already dying person. Even if additional cases could not be justified by the same logic which justified killing of, say, the terminally ill patient in great pain (for whom death is imminent and moral self-possession may be rapidly deteriorating); it is possible that attitudes toward the value of persons who are less productive or more expensive might be eroded, so that their lives would be placed at risk. A move might occur from rare and 'last resort' killing as in the interests of the person killed, to a general practice of killing those who are burdensome to others.

While this argument is important in considering the institution of social and medical policies, it does not satisfactorily resolve the morality of single cases of mercy-killing in which stipulated extreme conditions such as intractable pain and imminent death do obtain. The distinction between omission and commission is always morally *relevant*, since all things being equal, it is better to bring about a peaceful death by ceasing treatment than by killing. However, it is not absolutely clear that this distinction is in every case morally *decisive*. This is especially the case if, as Christian tradition has maintained, life is a conditional rather than an absolute value, and if continued biological life itself can threaten the higher spiritual and moral values for which it was created to serve as the condition. Justified instances of direct killing, if there are any, would certainly be rare, and of a borderline nature. They would arise only when circumstances present an acute affront to personal dignity, and possible only in those in which death is in any case impending. Such instances, even if justifiable, would never be without the aura of tragedy and ambiguity that surround all human decision-making in those situations in which we experience conflicts of our most esteemed and vital values.

It is because of a profound and irreducible ambiguity in any argument that personal suffering can justify human destruction of the life that only the Creator can bestow, that Christianity traditionally has evaluated mercy-killing as 'murder'. But, on the other hand, it is due to the recognition that temporal, biological life is finite and relative in value, that approval has been extended to those who in painful circumstances decline to pursue measures to sustain life.

On the whole, Christian tradition envisions life as a fundamental value but not an absolute one. This is why causing death can be a form of respect for life, and particularly for the total dignity and welfare of persons, which include spiritual as well as physical aspects. This same tradition has limited causation to indirect means although that limit is the subject of ongoing discussion among those who see relief of suffering as a duty of love which can in exceptional cases outweigh the stringent duty not to destroy life directly.

Notes

1. Pope Pius XII 'The Prolongation of Life', An Address to an International Congress of Anaesthesiologists, 24 November 1957, *The Pope Speaks* 4 (1957) pp. 395–396. See also *Acta Apostolicae Sedis* 49 (1957).

2. Richard A. McCormick 'To Save Or Let Die' *Journal of the American Medical Association* 229 (1974), 172–176. Published simultaneously in *America*, 17 July 1974.

3. *Ibid.* p. 174.

4. Gerald Kelly *Medical-Moral Problems* (St. Louis 1958) p. 123.

5. McCormick 'To Save Or Let Die' at p. 175.

6. 'Pastoral Constitution on the Church in the Modern World' Ch. II.27, in *The Documents of Vatican* II ed. Walter M. Abbott (New York 1966), p. 227.

7. Kelly *Medical-Moral Problems* p. 116.

8. Sacred Congregation for the Doctrine of the Faith *Declaration on Euthanasia*, 5 May 1980 (Boston 1980) p. 5. Reprinted from *L'Osservatore Romano*, English Edition.

9. *Ibid.* p. 9.

10. *Declaration on Euthanasia* p. 9.

11. *Declaration on Euthanasia* pp. 9–10.

12. Pope Pius XII 'Anesthesia: Three Moral Questions', Address to the Italian Society of Anaesthesiology, 24 February 1957, *The Pope Speaks* 4 (1957) pp. 33–50. See also *Acta Apostolicae Sedis* 49 (1957).

13. *Ibid.* p. 11.

14. Among the contributors to the development of the definition are St Alphonsus Liguouri, the Jesuit John De Lugo, the Dominicans Soto and Bannez, and more recently, the authors of the earlier twentieth-century manuals of moral theology, such as Buceroni, Aertnys-Damen, Capellman, Noldin-Schmidt, Jone-Adelman, Lehmkuhl and Kelly. For a historical summary, see Thomas J. O'Donnell *Medicine and Christian Morality* (New York 1976) pp. 47–55.

15. For a negative answer, see J. McCarthy 'Taking of Insulin to Preserve Life' *The Irish Ecclesiastical Record* 58 (1941) pp. 552–554. For a positive analysis, see G. Kelly 'The Duty of Using Artificial Means of Preserving Life' *Theological Studies* 12 (1951), pp. 550–556; and *Medical-Moral Problems* p. 130.

16. Richard A. McCormick 'Notes on Moral Theology: 1983' *Theological Studies* 45 (1984) pp. 115–119. See also three essays on cessation of intravenous feeding by Bonnie Steinbock, James Childress and Joanne Lynn, and Daniel Callahan, all in the *Hastings Center Report* 13 (October 1983).

Annemarie Pieper

Ethical Arguments in Favour of Suicide

1. ARGUMENTS FOR THE RIGHT TO COMMIT SUICIDE

(a) Exit Associations and Prominent Advocates

ALL OVER the world, in the last five years, organisations have been founded, calling for the recognition that every human being has the right to die with true human dignity. In Denmark: Mit Livstestamente. Retten til en voerdig død (1980); in Germany: Deutsche Gesellschaft für humanes Sterben (1981); in France: Association pour le Droit de Mourir dans la Dignité (1980); in Italy: Società Italiana di Tanatalogia (1979); in Canada: Dying with Dignity (1981) etc. Other societies have been in existence for longer, e.g., in Great Britain: EXIT—The Society for the Right to Die with Dignity (1935); in the USA: Concern for Dying (1967) and the America Euthanasia Foundation (1972) etc.

In addition to these exit-associations, numbering tens of thousands of members worldwide, which have organised themselves in order to be more effective in putting forward their claims, individual writers too have championed the individual's right to die with dignity. In 1985, in his book *Selbstmord und Selbstmordverhütung* the jurist Joachim Wagner put the case for the recognition of a 'constitutional right to suicide'. The writer Jean Améry wrote in his book *Hand an sich legen*, in 1976, 'Until . . . a movement is brought into being which urgently calls for the binding recognition that people have an inalienable right freely to choose to die, things will remain as they are' (62). Also in 1976, the philosopher Walter Kamlah, in his monograph *Meditatio mortis*, defends the view that 'it is morally permissible, on the basis of calm and mature deliberation, to relieve oneself of a life which has become intolerably burdensome, no longer yields fulfilment and has no

39

prospects of recovery' (24). In 1979, in her document *Freiwillig aus dem Leben* the artist Jo Roman confidently writes: 'I believe that the time will soon come when, as a result of awareness of the individual's personal responsibility for the length of his or her life—as well as for its content—it will be recognised that there is a basic human right freely and with deliberation to choose to die, and that it will be given the assistance and protection of society' (18).

(b) Suicide Instruction Manuals

Finally, the sociologists Claude Guillon and Yves Le Bonniec, in their provocatively-titled *Gebrauchsanleitung zum Selbstmord* (*The Suicide Instruction Manual*) (1982) put forward a 'polemic for the right to a freely chosen death', in which they accuse the inhuman power-structures of modern society of being responsible for the large numbers of suicides. As long as it is only the powerful and privileged who are able to lead a worthwhile life, whereas the others are obliged by the pressure of circumstance to accept a life which no longer deserves the name since it only brings them suffering, say Guillon and Le Bonniec, anyone who is no longer able to endure an existence unworthy of a human being must have access to the means to procure a peaceful death. So the authors see their recommendations, advice and hints concerning successful methods of suicide as practical information and assistance for those who have come to prefer death to life. This assistance consists in listing the various medicaments on the market—sleeping tablets, analgesics, tranquillisers, antihistamines, antidepressants, cardiac preparations etc., and giving the appropriate number of tablets or ampoules regarded as the minimum fatal dosage. They also describe the way in which each works and advise against taking substances which cause unbearably severe pain (194). They recommend that one should book a room in a hotel, 'paying two days in advance and telling the hotel staff that you do not want to be disturbed for those two days' (195).

> You should have a light meal, so that your stomach is not too empty, otherwise it will react over-sensitively to the huge dose, but it must not be too full. To minimise the danger of being sick, you can take sea-sickness tablets shortly before the meal and about one hour before taking the fatal dose. It is advisable to have tested the effectiveness of these anti-sickness tablets beforehand (195f.). To avoid being brought back to life against your will, you must take care to destroy the packages and containers of the medicaments used. You must also destroy . . . any documents which might implicate anyone else in taking part, deliberately or by neglect, in setting up the suicide (212f.).

(c) Suicide as a Right of Resistance

These instructions strike one as cynical. But the cynicism is directed against a society characterised by totalitarian power-claims and the intense pressure to show achievement, reducing the individual's autonomy and responsibility to a minimum as a result of systems of compulsion which have no regard for man. Such a society is unmasked as the real murderer. Guillon and Le Bonniec by no means wish to make wanton profit out of others' misfortune; on the contrary, one senses that they are angry and appalled at the waste of so much life, life that could be lived (37)—if circumstances were otherwise and if men would stop oppressing other men. What Guillon and Le Bonniec are urging from the perspective of social criticism, i.e., the right to suicide as a kind of right of resistance against society, Jean Améry, Walter Kamlah and Jo Roman have demanded from the point of view of the individual who is suffering either from his environment or from a terminal illness. Not only have the latter defended the individual's right to die with human dignity: they have also put it forward as their justification for taking their own lives.

(d) The Main Arguments: Death with Dignity and the Realisation of Freedom

Spokespersons for the right to suicide base this right, on the one hand, on the right to die with human dignity, and on the other hand, on human freedom. In his 'Apology for suicide' Améry's starting-point is that to choose death is 'a privilege of being human' (52); i.e., only the human being, endowed with reason, can take his or her own life. Only a being which can distance itself from itself and thus evaluate itself critically, is in a position to envisage a more desirable alternative than a life-process which runs on merely naturally. Only such a being can ask the question which Améry puts: '*Must we live?* Must we exist, simply because we happen to be?' (24). In other words: can we conclude that we ought to exist simply from the fact that we actually do exist? Améry denies this, asserting that 'the subject's option is what counts' (154) and not the objective state of affairs. Heavily condensed, his argument is this: If it is a basic fact that the human being belongs essentially to himself (105), and that he is entitled to dispose of his most personal possession, i.e., himself, then he also has the right to destroy this possession—provided that in doing so he is escaping from 'a life without dignity, humanity and freedom' (154). This flight from the absurdity of existence into the absurdity of nothingness (55) as a result of disgust with life (56), according to Améry, is an act involving both a denial and an affirmation. 'What is suicide, considered as a natural death, but the blasting refusal to accept the blasting, crushing negativity of existence?' (69). The nihil-principle takes the place of the hope-principle (61), and utters a radical No to a life which has become meaningless. For Améry, however, a freely chosen death is 'much more than the pure act of self-liquidation' (83) or a private ultimate solution. In the protest against an unbearable life without meaning there is also a Yes; a Yes to the idea of a life without loneliness, hostility and compulsion, or, to put it positively; a Yes to life in freedom and peace. According to Améry, a person who deliberately chooses to end his life is actually realising some part of that freedom which life has shown to be impossible; thus this most extreme use of life, which is in fact an ultimate misuse, is not only an act of total destruction but, as an act of liberation, also contains a positive element. Améry explains this by an analogy: 'In the same way, the piece of wood in the hands of the carver does not remain itself. It becomes a negation of mere wood. And since liberation is destruction, it finds its ultimate reaffirmation in a self-chosen death' (130). Améry does not even exclude the possibility that, despite all the destructivity involved, 'in taking our own life, when our I is lost in self-extinction and realises itself totally—perhaps for the first time—a hitherto unknown happiness' may be experienced (79). For Améry, therefore, suicide represents a triumph of freedom over all the heteronomous compulsions which hold sway over man.

> In the lived world, with his 'I', and as an 'I', man is free; that is, he experiences himself as free and acts, and must act, as if he were free. . . . We could not exist for so much as an hour if we were to wait to see where the causal chain would carry us. We are subject; yet we experience ourselves as free (140).

Kamlah, too, sees self-chosen death as a legitimate act of liberation on the part of the human being, although his argument runs in a rather different direction. Man can only take responsibility for something, in an absolute sense, if he is free to choose it and able to recognise it as binding. But, argues Kamlah, 'no one consulted me when I came into the world; consequently I cannot be compelled to stay in it if my life has become a burden to me and to others' (19). Freedom, as understood by Kamlah, is the ability to determine a process which has come about without my cooperation, yet which can be terminated by me as a result of my free will.

2. THE ETHICAL ARGUMENTS DISCUSSED

(a) The Issues and the Premisses of an Answer

The proponents of a right to suicide quote the principle of freedom in support of their claim that suicide has the dignity of a human right. They want their arguments to be understood as *moral* grounds which every rational being ought to regard as generally binding in practice. So the question arises: Can such a claim to morality be actually substantiated in the case of suicide? Can ethics provide a foundation for the human right to end one's life? I would like to preface my observations on these questions with two premises: In the first place I am putting forward my theses within the framework of a *philosophical* ethics ultimately based on a moral principle immanent in human reason, i.e., not dependent upon a concept of God. Ethics, as a study of the conditions of the morality of human action, does not ignore or deny God; morality is required of everyone, irrespective of his personal religious behaviour (or lack of it), and so ethics simply assumes that a divine will is not necessary to substantiate moral demands. In the second place I am presupposing that suicide is not in every case pathological, the tragic end of something which is felt to be totally determined by external or internal forces, as A. Alvarez describes in his book *The Savage·God*:

> My life felt so cluttered and obstructed that I could hardly breathe. I inhabited a closed, concentrated world, airless and without exits. . . . I had entered the closed world of suicide and my life was being lived for me by forces I couldn't control (227.)

A person who takes his or her own life in such a sick condition is not really the agent of death, but is only functioning as the tool of a stronger, dominating power. Campaigners for the freedom to take one's own life are not arguing that this group of pathological potential suicides, who doubtless need medical help, should be given this right. They are concerned with those who—like Améry, Kamlah and Roman—knowingly and willingly administer death to *themselves* and understand it as a free act.

(b) No Right, but Permission

What then can be said about ethical arguments for the right to end one's own life? In what follows I want to try to substantiate the thesis that man— from an ethical point of view—has no *right* to suicide, but he *is permitted* to kill himself. If suicide is a permissible act, it follows that, while we have no right to it, suicide is not wrong either. To explain this, I must first of all say that ethics has developed a special discipline within logic, the so-called deontic logic or logic of norms, which concerns itself with the structure of normative statements in the sense of an ethical modal logic. Analogously to the operators of modal logic, i.e., possible, impossible, necessary, the operators of deontic logic are: permitted, forbidden, commanded. Accordingly, an action is permitted when it is neither commanded not forbidden. I want to show that suicide belongs to the class of morally permitted actions, with the consequences this has for the evaluation of suicide. The first step is to show that suicide can be neither commanded nor forbidden morally. The second step will be to try to define the notion of 'permission' with regard to suicide as against the concept of 'right'.

(c) Suicide is neither Commanded nor Forbidden

From the point of view of ethics, therefore, suicide can be neither commanded nor forbidden. *From the point of view of ethics*; for there have been and are de facto moral codes which command suicide and also those which forbid it. Thus, for instance, the ancient Eskimo morality regarded suicide as the norm for old people who were no longer able to provide for their keep. The justification for this norm was that, with the most meagre resources and a restricted work-capacity, this was the only way to ensure the survival of the group. There is an analogy in ritual or religious self-sacrifice, which is intended to ensure the common good, or else to be a response to the divine will, and is thus commanded. Other moral codifications, like the Decalogue, for instance, forbid suicide under pain of the death-penalty on the grounds that, by doing so, man transgresses against the divine will. For ethics, however, not everything that is recognised and practised within a particular group or community is automatically a *valid* moral norm. The fact that norms operate is not a sufficient basis, as far as ethics is concerned, for their morality. If what is normative, justified and meaningful for and within one group of people, is to be shown to be unconditionally valid, it must be capable of generalisation. But if the command or the interdiction of suicide is generalised, i.e., if one says that whenever situation X occurs, suicide is commanded for everyone in that situation, or that suicide is always forbidden under all circumstances, both norms are clearly inhumane. No universally valid norm can be established obliging everyone to commit suicide in a particular situation—for example, anyone who is taken prisoner is morally obliged to commit suicide if that is the only way to be sure of saving the lives of others, whose names might be extracted from him under torture. Nor can one simply forbid suicide absolutely, for to do so would be to imply, positively, that everyone is obliged to go on living, under all circumstances and at any cost, as long as he lives. Each of these demands is an inhumane as the other; both the command and the interdiction of suicide restrict human freedom in a way that is ethically inadmissible.

(d) The Ultimate Good: not Life, but Freedom

But we must be more precise; it must be shown that, ethically considered, it is not life, but freedom which is the ultimate human good. Here, freedom does not mean subjective arbitrariness, but moral freedom, i.e., the freedom which is aware that it is always related to the freedom of others, freely limiting itself for the sake of the freedom of all by means of the principle of generalisation. It is this self-limiting freedom, which in doing so facilitates the freedom of all, which is the final and normative standard for all human conduct. It is not the fact that man is alive that makes him human, for from a purely natural, biological point of view, plants and animals are also alive; indeed, every organic being exists. Life is a necessary, but not a sufficient, condition for being human. What is sufficient for man to exist as man, i.e., in accord with his human dignity, is freedom. Only as a free living being is man completely human.

(e) A Middle Position: the Realisation of Freedom involves the Possibility of Suicide

What then are the implications of this ethical definition of man for the problem of suicide? If the meaning of human life does not consist in simply living, but in living as a human being and according to the standards of moral freedom, man does not exist primarily for the sake of life, but in order to exercise freedom. Now the question arises, does the exercise of freedom, which constitutes man as man, also include the possibility of his putting an end to his own life, of his actively bringing death upon himself, instead of waiting until it catches up with him of its own accord? From the point of view of ethics, even if only as an exception, a peripheral instance of human freedom, I want to affirm this possibility and put forward the thesis that suicide is a permissible act, an act which is thus morally possible—not morally necessary and not morally impossible either. An act which is morally neither commanded nor prohibited, which is optional, occupies a middle position as a permitted act since it does not violate the principle of freedom as do prohibited actions, nor does it reaffirm this principle as do actions that are commanded, which facilitate freedom in a fundamental sense. Suicide, provided that it is not pathological, but well-considered, is an act performed for the sake of freedom. Certainly it does not open up any new freedom for the person concerned; it removes for ever this way of being human; but the act plainly shows that it does not want the principle of freedom to be deprived of its validity: on the contrary, it recognises this principle, and because it does so, it prefers death to a life that is not free and hence no longer worthy of the human being, a life that is unworthy of life. A life that can only be lived by sacrificing humanity is less than, and less worthy of man, than mere non-existence.

(f) Kant's 'facultas moralis' and the Ethical Borderline Case

With the help of the terminology applied by Immanuel Kant in his *Metaphysics of Morals*, I would now like to bring together what I have said about the ethical modal categories of the commanded, the forbidden and the permitted. Then, by way of conclusion, I shall go on to examine the consequences of suicide considered as a permitted act. Kant's formula for commanded acts is: 'Obligation is the necessity of a free act in accord with a categorical imperative on the part of reason' (327). In other words, if it is to be demanded unconditionally and morally, an act must be autonomous, i.e., subject to a universal law and thus acknowledging a norm which freedom itself has undertaken to observe (the moral law) as absolutely binding. Thus we are obliged to respect the principle of freedom always and unconditionally. Analogously, an act is forbidden if it transgresses against the law of freedom or actually tries to replace the principle of freedom by the principle of unfreedom. According to Kant, an act is permitted if 'it is not opposed to obligation; and this freedom, which is not restricted by any opposing imperative, is an authorised freedom (*facultas moralis*); (328). Kant goes on:

> An act that is neither commanded nor forbidden is merely *permitted*, since, with regard to it, there is no law which might limit freedom, and hence no obligation either. Such an act is termed morally indifferent (*indifferens, adiaophoron, res merae facultatis*). The question can be asked, whether there are such acts (329).

Elsewhere Kant explicitly denies, from the ethical point of view, that there can be this category of permitted acts (and hence the moral possibility of suicide), since there is no middle ground between good and evil, and all moral acts must fall into one of the two classes, as actions that are either commanded or forbidden (*Die Religion* 21f. footnote). It can be properly objected, however, that, beside morally commanded and forbidden acts, there is a large class of acts that are neither good nor evil, yet are not meaningless and aimless as a result, although they are not directly subject to the moral law. This large class of optional or permitted acts, e.g., games, and subjective decisions like the choice of clothes, a holiday location or a friend, is not on a par with the class of commanded and forbidden acts, but subordinate to it, in so far as it too is ultimately bound to the principle of freedom. All the same, it represents a special class of acts, of which suicide is a borderline case.

3. CONSEQUENCES OF THE THESIS THAT SUICIDE IS PERMISSIBLE

What follows from the fact that an act is permissible? By contrast with an act that is commanded, in which case I *must* act in order to do my duty, permission means that I *can* act, but am not obliged to. Applied to suicide this means that I may myself put an end to a life which has become meaningless for me, which is no longer marked by human dignity, but I am not obliged to do so. I can decide this way or that, since, as with all permitted acts, both alternatives are indifferent, equally valid. In other words, this is not a case of Yes *or* No, but Yes *and* No. Permitted acts are morally indifferent, not prescribed; they are not so related to the moral law that they are predetermined, they do not imply a Yes or No to a command or a prohibition. If, therefore, someone freely decides to choose death, he is not exceeding the bounds of morality, but stopping at the moral frontier—albeit in a way that is final.

(a) No Right to Suicide

The person who commits suicide is not acting immorally. But we cannot conclude from this that he has a right to suicide. A right, ethically, is always correlated with an obligation; i.e., we can only speak of rights in relation to acts which are enjoined upon everyone, acts which are commanded. For example, the right to truth enjoins everyone to direct his thoughts and actions according to the command of truth. The same applies to freedom, justice, human dignity and all that justly claims unqualified validity. But with regard to the right to life we must distinguish: for no one has a right to life in the sense that he has an unconditional claim to be begotten. Once human beings exist, however, they have a right to exist as human beings, that is, with human dignity. To this right there corresponds the duty of doing one's utmost to make such an existence possible. Only when such a life has become impossible, for reasons which the individual does not have to bring forward, and when the relevant right no longer seems realisable, even on a long time-scale, only then is the obligation to live extinguished. The alternatives of carrying on living despite everything, or of taking one's life, are ethically equal possibilities. For they no longer occupy contrary and irreconcilable positions at the level of rights and obligations, but fall under the category of permitted actions, where suicide is defined as morally indifferent and hence admissible, without establishing a right to suicide.

(b) No Moral Condemnation

If it is the case that suicide, ethically speaking, is permissible, without this implying a right to suicide, there are two substantial consequences. The first concerns those who reject suicide: no one should pronounce moral condemnation on a person who commits suicide, or otherwise speak ill of him, whether his condition is pathological—in which case he is not responsible anyway—or whether he puts an end to his life freely, of his own accord—for then he is carrying out something morally permissible. Where there is no right, but only permission, there is no judge. Hence the 1954 judgment of the Federal German Court ought to be corrected, for it says: 'All suicide—apart, perhaps, from the most exceptional cases—is strongly disapproved of by the moral law, for no one may assume the power to dispose of his own life and administer death to himself' (*Entscheidungen des Bundesgerichtshofs in Strafsachen*, vol. 6, p. 153).

(c) But no Positive Regulation either

The second consequence applies to those who advocate suicide: there is no right to suicide, and the mere fact that it is permissible does not suffice to provide a measure of regulation and institutionalisation for it. When, in *Freiwillig aus dem Leben* Jo Roman suggests that the Government should set up a 'Federal Commission on Freely Chosen Death' which would provide guidelines, 'developing a model for a dignified death by suicide or euthanasia' (211), and when she goes on to suggest the establishment of so-called Exit Houses, places where people who want to die can do so, one is gruesomely reminded of the death-clinic in Aldous Huxley's futuristic novel *Brave New World*. Furthermore, she is engaging in the futile attempt to regulate something which eludes and is bound to elude all regulation. For the category of the permissible cannot yield a bill of rights, nor a summons to commit suicide, nor propaganda for an act of this kind, which is only permitted as an exception and hence must be left to the personal decision of the individual.

Translated by Graham Harrison

Literature

A. Alvarez *The Savage God* A Study of Suicide (London 1972)

J. Améry *Hand an sich legen. Diskurs über den Freitod* (Stuttgart 1976)

C. Guillon and Y. Le Bonniec *Gebrauchsanleitung zum Selbstmord. Eine Streitschrift für das Recht auf einen frei bestimmten Tod* (Frankfurt 1982)

W. Kamlah *Meditatio mortis. Kann man den Tod 'verstehen', und gibt es ein 'Recht auf den eigenen Tod'?* (Stuttgart 1976)

I. Kant *Die Metaphysik der Sitten* (*Foundations of the Metaphysics of Morals*)

I. Kant *Die Religion innerhalb der Grenzen der blossen Vernunft* (*Religion within the Limits of Reason Alone*)

J. Roman *Freiwillig aus dem Leben. Ein Dokument* (Munich 1981)

J. Wagner *Selbstmord und Selbstmordverhütung* (Karlsruhe 1975)

Paula Caucanas-Pisier

Associations for the Right to Die in Dignity

1. GENERAL

(a) Historical

IT SEEMS that the oldest society formed to defend the right to die in dignity is the English society, the V.E.S.,[1] founded exactly fifty years ago in 1935. Of course it is the best known one, at least in Europe, because for the last few years it has adopted the striking name of EXIT. The way in which one of its vice-presidents, the writer Arthur Koestler and his wife, decided to die together on 3 March 1983 also gained it world headlines. But one of the societies existing in the United States is almost as venerable, since it was founded in 1938. In fact there were probably more or less formal groups in existence even before this or in the years that followed, but they have disappeared without trace or been taken over by more recent societies.

At any rate, we have to wait more than thirty years for the foundation, one after another, in 1972 and 1973, of two more societies in the United States (A.E.F. and C.F.D.). A large number of societies were formed during the seventies: in 1973, one in Australia, two in Holland and one in Sweden; in 1974, one in South Africa and another in Australia; in 1975, a third one in Holland; in 1976, one in Denmark and one in Japan; in 1977, one in Norway; in 1978, two in New Zealand; in 1979, one in Colombia. That is thirteen societies founded between 1973 and 1979.

1. For the meaning of abbreviations, see the list of Associations at the end of the article.

The number of societies has grown even more quickly since the beginning of the eighties; fourteen societies have been founded in less than five years. In 1980 a third one was founded in Australia, one in W. Germany, a fourth one in the US, one in Scotland and one in France; in 1981, one in India; in 1982, two in Belgium (one French-speaking and one Flemish), two in Canada (one in the West and another in the East), a second one in England, two in Switzerland (one German and one French-speaking); in 1984, one in Spain. Two societies are in the process of formation in Brazil and Poland, and probably in many other countries there are more or less official groups, which have not yet reached national status or felt the need to make themselves known at international level.

Of course these societies are very different from each other and we will return to these differences. But it was inevitable that the speed and size of their increase led them to feel the need to find out about each other and give mutual support, even to meet and form groups. The first international meeting of this kind took place in Tokyo in 1976, the second in San Francisco in 1978. It became necessary to set up a World Federation: its provisions were laid down at the third international conference at Oxford (England) in 1980. Thus the World Federation of Right-to-Die Societies was formed and its first president was Sidney Rosoff. Its statutes were ratified at the fourth international conference at Melbourne (Australia) in 1982. Tim Saclier (Australia) became its second president. The fifth international conference took place at Nice (France) in 1984: twenty-six associations (not all the existing societies are affiliated to the World Federation) representing nearly 500,000 members took part and M. R. Masani (India) became president. This conference had considerable international press coverage. This was increased in France by the publication, a few days beforehand, of a poll conducted by a medical journal (*Tonus*) showing that 81 per cent of French doctors were in favour of euthanasia for hopeless incurable disease and by the publication of a manifesto, in which five doctors declared that they were prepared to consider with their patients, at these patients' request, the matter of death and to work out with them the means of providing them with an end to life as free from pain and anxiety as possible. They also stated that they had already helped patients with terminal diseases to end their lives in the least unpleasant possible conditions.

(b) The Medical Question

It appears that the first factor leading to the appearance of these various societies was the problem caused, both for patient and doctor, by the suffering accompanying the terminal phases of a mortal disease. This is why the word euthanasia always appears in the titles or the aims of the oldest societies: they affirm the right to voluntary euthanasia. In countries like the USA or South Africa, where legislation is particularly strict on doctors, who are often taken to court even for less drastic interventions, it is a matter of giving doctors who agree to their patients' demands for euthanasia guarantees against possible legal proceedings.

This is why many of these associations are trying to get recognition for a will (given different names: in France it is called a 'biological will'), in which the testator declares that he or she does not wish to go on living under certain (specified) conditions, requires kin, doctors and nursing personnel to respect this wish and discharges their responsibility in advance. This procedure is strongly disapproved of by some but the need for such a will is recognised in one way or another by nearly all the associations. They distribute specimen documents to their members and keep copies of any such wills made in their archives. In the United States, where legislation varies from one state to another in this as in other matters, the legislatures of 23 states have recognised the legal status of such documents (*Living will legislations*). In countries where the practice of medicine leads to fewer legal actions than in the US, such a will only has the value which the family and care staff are willing to accord it. So the various associations are also trying, when legal recognition for such wills is not forthcoming, to create a climate of opinion which would exert moral pressure on people to respect them.

Of course this problem is connected with the state of medical practice. Where there is little medical intervention in humann lives, people die 'naturally'. Now that—in some parts of the world—there is a lot more medical intervention, two situations are possible. Either the medical intervention causes a substantial improvement and the patient has a new lease of life of higher quality. Or the intervention fails or is not possible but medicine prevents the death that, of its own accord, would come quite quickly, and the patient is given a new lease of life of a more or less inferior quality. In the fifty years since the first associations were founded, the extraordinary progress of medicine has multiplied the number of cures and cases of happy old age. Medicine has also increased the number of people who survive in conditions which are sometimes very painful.

This explains why the large majority of members of these associations are not doctors, nurses, lawyers, politicians, social workers etc., who have to deal with these problems, but ordinary men and women, usually over fifty or sixty, who do not wish to go on living in conditions which, rightly or wrongly, they regard as intolerable.

Contrary to what is often thought, the majority of members are not from the 'middle' and 'upper' classes but from the 'working' class. Moreover a substantial number of members have already been in pain for a long time and put up bravely with a difficult life, but refuse to go beyond a certain level of suffering and degradation. So it is not a question of cowardice but of dignity. Often they are women (there are more women than men in these age groups) who have nursed their husbands or parents, sometimes through a long and painful illness, till death and who do not wish to impose such a burden (and such an image of themselves!) upon others. Of course the associations also include doctors, nurses, lawyers, social workers, 'intellectuals' interested in these problems, but their main strength—quantitatively and qualitatively—is in the accumulated experience of all their members and the needs arising from this experience.

(c) Expansion of the Problem

During the last decade there has been an important development in the state of the problem and this has been expressed in a change of vocabulary appearing in these societies' programmes and sometimes the choice of a new official title. The word 'euthanasia' is tending to disappear to be replaced by the expression 'right to die in dignity' (or, more succinctly in English: right to die). Some people see this change of vocabulary as a more or less hypocritical coverup, which once again hides the reality of death in our modern world. In fact it is something quite different.

Firstly it makes a certain demedicalisation of the problem. Whether active or passive, euthanasia is a medical *problem*, discussed and judged by doctors, and it is always a medical *act*. But most members of these societies think that many other factors besides the medical enter into the judgment a person should make on his or her own life and death: emotional, family, economic, psychological or even physiological aspects which can be considered as illnesses (blindness, deafness, impotence, paralysis, incontinence etc . . .) but are not of course medical indications for euthanasia. Thus the problem is no longer confined to the terminal stage of incurable diseases and the members of these societies refuse to hand over to doctors—even the most sympathetic and co-operative—a responsibility they believe is primarily their own.

At the same time this demedicalisation is accompanied by a reappropriation of their death by the living. They no longer want their death to belong to the authorities, medical or otherwise. They believe their death is theirs, and they are responsible for it, as they have been for all the other things in their lives. Because they have tried to live with dignity they want to die with dignity. Because death is part of life they want to take charge of their death as they have tried to take charge of their life. However this does not of course eliminate a medical side to the problem, which is inevitable: dying in dignity often requires a doctor's help, or at least the resort to medicaments, which are not freely on sale and the dosage of which is in the hands of experts. This does not make it a substantially medical problem dependent solely or primarily on the doctor's judgment. As Arthur Koestler put it more or less: we needed doctors, at least midwives to be born (then to live well) and we have also needed them to die well. But this indisputable necessity does not prove that entry into and departure from life are essentially medical choices, over which doctors should have sole control. It is not accidental that it is often the same people in these associations who have endeavoured to promote responsible fertility and parenthood and who want to promote the conditions for a responsible death. And just as in the one case the people concerned (primarily of course women) had to unite and act to make the medical and other authorities move, so the men and women directly concerned, who wish to be able to die in dignity, have had to unite and act to force the relevant authorities to move.

One thing that many of these societies do is to supply their members, under rigorous control, with booklets or pamphlets giving detailed information on the various techniques leading to an easy death. In many countries this is impossible because their laws regard the distribution of such literature as incitement to suicide, which is an offence or crime in these countries. Most associations try to put pressure on the authorities to gain a modification of such legislation. They also often become involved in trials of people brought to court for helping someone to procure an easy death: members of the family, nursing staff, doctors etc. . . . . On the other hand some of the associations are much more cautious about offering direct help: nearly all of them refuse to offer such help to die on their own account. They are associations for dying in dignity not for inciting people to commit suicide.

(d) Geographical and Cultural Expansion

A glance at the brief history at the beginning of the article shows that these societies appeared first in countries with two characteristics: (i) a fairly high standard of living, (ii) a Protestant tradition. The medical and economic aspects of the problem suffice to explain the first characteristic, and religious and cultural history offers an explanation for the second.

But on these points there has also been a noticeable development. Even apart from the special case of Japan (a society founded in 1976, the members of which include leading doctors, journalists and M.P.s), a society was founded in 1979 in Colombia, which is both a Catholic and a relatively under-developed country; its founder is not an enthusiast or a visionary but a leading doctor, administrator and politician: Dr Cesar Augusto Pentoja, who is also an official member of the government council of medical ethics. In 1981 a society was founded in India: here again a leading political figure, M. R. Masani, is the president. He is also the current president of the World Federation. In 1980 a society was founded in France, a country with a 90 per cent Catholic tradition, 'the Church's eldest daughter'. In 1982 two societies were founded in Belgium, also a country with a Catholic tradition. Societies are also in the process of formation in Brazil and Poland. Thus we see that these societies are no longer confined to so-called developed countries. It is easy to explain this as an effect of the fact that medical progress and the enormous increase in life expectancy are no longer confined to these developed countries either. But the societies are also no longer confined to countries with a Protestant or 'charismatic' tradition.

It is true that in countries with a Catholic tradition, these societies mainly recruit their members from among Protestants, freemasons, agnostics, rationalists, free thinkers and more or less militant atheists. But we know that they also contain a not insignificant and ever growing number of Catholics. Some will see this as a sign that Catholicism is weakening its hold upon its flock or in these countries. We do not think we are in a position to judge this. But we know that many of our Catholic members—like many of their Protestant brothers and sisters—think that human beings do not insult God more by wanting to die in dignity than by wanting to live in dignity. The Scottish society, for example, has made a point of announcing that it does not think of itself as necessarily atheist or free thinking. An American society has as its president an eminent biblical scholar, archaeologist and historian. It has on its committee a professor of law of the Loyola Law School. Lord Cogan, the former Archbishop of Canterbury, always refused to disapprove of active euthanasia and an Anglican archbishop wondered what people would think in a hundred years' time of Christians today who allow human beings to die in a way they would not dare allow animals to. We leave to others more competent to judge whether this archbishop is a good Christian or not for holding such views.

2. LIST OF SOCIETIES

(known to the World Federation or affiliated to it).

(a) Africa

South Africa Voluntary Euthanasia Society (S.A.V.E.S.)
P.O. Box 37141, Overport 4067, Durban, Republic of South Africa.
Founded in 1974. About 8,000 members. Has published a twice yearly bulletin since 1977: *S.A.V.E.S.*

(b) America

CANADA
(i) Dying with Dignity (West)
P.O. Box 46408, Station 8, Vancouver, British Columbia V6R 4G7, Canada.
(ii) Dying with Dignity (East)
175 St Clair Avenue West, Toronto, Ontario M4V 1P7, Canada.
Founded in 1982. About 400 members.

COLOMBIA
Funacion Pro-Derecho a Morir Dignamente (D.M.D.)
Apartado Aereo 89314, Bogota, Colombia.
Founded in 1979. About 2,300 members.

UNITED STATES
(i) American Euthanasia Foundation
95 North Birch Road, Suite 301, Fort Lauderdale, Florida 33304, USA.
Founded in 1972. About 30,000 members.
(ii) Concern for Dying
250 West 57th Street, New York, NY 10107, USA.
Founded in 1967. About 270,000 members. For six years has published quarterly bulletin: *Concern for Dying* and numerous pamphlets. Has published a book: *Euthanasia, a Decade of Change*, Excerpts from Annual Conferences, 1968–1977.
(iii) Hemlock Society
P.O. Box 66218, Los Angeles, California 90066, USA.
Founded in 1980. About 10,000 members. Publishes quarterly bulletin: *Hemlock Quarterly*.
(iv) Society for the Right to Die
250 West 57th Street, New York, NY 10107, USA.
Founded in 1938. About 70,000 members.

(c) Asia

INDIA
The Society for the Right to Die with Dignity
Maneckjee Wadia Bldg, 4th Floor, 127 Mahatma Gandhi Road, Fort, Bombay 400 001, India.
Founded in 1981. About 200 members. Publishes a bulletin.

JAPAN
Japan Society for Dying with Dignity
Hamaso Building 1-11, Ogawa Machi, Kanda, Chiyoda Ku, Tokyo, Japan, N0101.
Founded in 1976. About 2,500 members. Publishes a bulletin periodically.

(d) Europe

WEST GERMANY
Deutsche Gesellschaft für Humanes Sterben (D.G.H.S.)
Postfach 11 05 29. 8900 Augsburg 11 W. Germany.
Founded in 1980. About 10,000 members. Publishes a twice yearly bulletin: *Humanes Leben, Humanes Sterben.*

ENGLAND
(i) The Voluntary Euthanasia Society (V.E.S.)
13 Prince of Wales Terrace, London W8 5PG, UK.
Founded in 1938. About 9,000 members (ex-EXIT). Publishes a twice yearly bulletin: *V.E.S. Newsletter.*
(ii) New Exit
50 South Hill Park, Hampstead, London NW3, UK.
Founded in 1982 as a breakaway group from the V.E.S. About 100 members. Distributes the bulletin of the Australian Society V.E.S.V.

BELGIUM
(i) Association pour le Droit de Mourir dans la Dignité
84 rue de la Pastorales B-1080 Brussels, Belgium.
Founded in 1982. About 100 members. Publishes a quarterly bulletin.
(ii) Vereniging voor Recht op Waardi Sterven (R.W.S.)
45 Somersstraat, 2018 Antwerp, Belgium.
Founded in 1982.

DENMARK
Mit Livstestamente—retten til en voerdig død
Jaegersborgvej 68, 2800 Lyngby, Denmark.
Founded in 1976. About 14,000 members.

SCOTLAND
The Voluntary Euthanasia Society for Scotland (V.E.S.S.)
17 Hart Street, Edinburgh EH1 3RO, Scotland, UK.
Founded in 1980. About 1,600 members. Publishes a twice yearly bulletin: *V.E.S.S. Newsletter.*

SPAIN
Associacion Derecho a Morir Dignamente (D.M.D.)
Apartado 9,094, 28080 Madrid, Spain.
Founded in 1984. Publishes a quarterly bulletin.

FRANCE
Association pour le Droit de Mourir dans la Dignité (A.D.M.D.)
103 rue La Fayette, 75010 Paris, France.
Founded in 1980. About 12,000 members. Publishes a twice yearly bulletin.

NORWAY
Landsforeningen mit Livstestament Retten til en verdig Død
Majorstuveien 35 B, Oslo 3, Norway.
Founded in 1977. About 650 members.

NETHERLANDS
(i) Nederlandse Vereniging voor Vrijwillige Euthanasia (N.V.V.V.E.)
Postbus 5331, 1007 AH, Amsterdam, Netherlands.
Founded in 1973. About 20,000 members. Publishes a quarterly bulletin: *V.E.*
(Vrijwillige Euthanasia).
(ii) Informatie Centrum Vrijwillige Euthanasia (I.C.V.E.)
Zuiderweg 42, 8393 KT Vinkega, Netherlands.
Founded in 1975. About 6,000 members. Publishes a bulletin: *Euthanatos*.
(iii) Stichting Vrijwillige Euthanasia (S.V.E.)
P.O. Box 85843, 2508 CM 's Gravenhage, Netherlands.
Founded in 1973. No members because it is not an association but a research
centre.

SWEDEN
Ratten Till Var Død (R.T.V.D.)
Linnegatan 7, 114 47 Stockholm, Sweden.
Founded in 1973. About 8,000 members.

SWITZERLAND
(i) Exit-Deutsche Schweiz Vereinigung für Humanes Sterben
Limmattalstrasse 177, CH 8049 Zürich, Switzerland.
Founded in 1982. About 3,900 members.
(ii) Exit-A.D.M.D. (Association pour le Droit de Mourir dans la Dignité)
Case postale 100, 1222 Vesenaz, Geneva, Switzerland.
Founded in 1982. About 1,000 members.

(*d*) Australasia

AUSTRALIA
(i) Voluntary Euthanasia Society of New South Wales
P.O. Box 25, Broadway, New South Wales 2007, Australia.
Founded in 1973. About 700 members. Publishes a quarterly bulletin: *V.E.S. New South Wales Newsletter.*
(ii) Voluntary Euthanasia Society of Victoria (V.E.S.V.)
P.O. Box 71, Mooroolbark, Victoria 3138, Australia.
Founded in 1974. About 1,000 members. Publishes a bulletin peridoically: *V.E.S.V. Report.*
(ii) West Australia Voluntary Euthanasia Society (W.A.V.E.S.)
P.O. Box 7243, Cloisters Square, Perth 6000, Australia.
Founded in 1980. About 500 members. Publishes a twice yearly bulletin: *WAVES News.*

NEW ZEALAND
(i) Voluntary Euthanasia Society
95 Melrose Road, Island Bay, Wellington 2, New Zealand.
Founded in 1978. About 250 members. Publishes a bulletin: *Newsletter.*
(ii) Voluntary Euthanasia Society (Auckland) Inc.
P.O. Box 77029, Mount Albert 3, Auckland, New Zealand.
Founded in 1978. About 500 members.

Translated by Dinah Livingstone

PART II

Theological Reflection

Niceto Blázquez

The Church's Traditional Moral Teaching on Suicide

SUICIDE IS the act by which a person directly, knowingly and freely brings about his or her own death. This study is not concerned with those suicides that moral theologians call indirect, nor with those persons who take their own lives in a state of mental abnormality or who cannot be held responsible for their actions.

1. AN OVERALL VIEW OF THE QUESTION

The Church's moral teaching and canonical discipline are basically inspired by biblical revelation, which holds all life without exception to be a gift from God the creator and an object of special predilection by Christ as redeemer. Man, therefore, is not the ultimate guardian of his life. He is only a faithful and watchful custodian of it, and has to give an account of his custodianship to God. The society into which Christianity burst, however, was one in which suicide was idealised and even counselled as a heroic act of human virtue. It saw man as tied basically not to God, but to the State, while at the same time proclaiming his absolute autonomy by recommending suicide, either as a lesser evil when faced with the demands of the State and the hardships of life, or simply as a proud affirmation of human self-sufficiency. This was the mentality of many important Greek and Roman philosophers and sages at the time when Christianity made its appearance on the historical scene.

Christian moral thinking on suicide reached its culmination in the teaching of St Augustine. His thought was later codified and enriched in the thirteenth century by St Thomas Aquinas, who has become the central and indispensable reference point for all Catholic moral theologians down to our own day. The first Christian moralists were primarily concerned with refuting the Stoic and Epicurean views that favoured suicide. St Augustine was forced to consider the matter by the terrorist commandos known as '*circunceliones*', who sometimes took their own lives as an extremist form of provocation to violence. In St Thomas' day, suicide was again current among Albigensians and Cathars. In the nineteenth century, Romanticism in its poetical, philosophical and sociological manifestations again idealised suicide, and in our own times it is once more becoming alarmingly prevalent with the growing materialism of present-day culture. The radicalised political activism and recourse to alienatory drugs practised by many young people produce new motives for suicide in the face of a future culturally closed to the transcendental values that can engender hope.

Alongside the Church's moral teaching on suicide, there is its canonical discipline on the subject to consider. This is to some extent already formulated in the Canons of the Apostles, and culminates in the *Codex* of 1917, via the *Corpus juris* and the Ritual. Today there are those who believe that canonical discipline against suicides has been too severe from the pastoral point of view, at least in theory. Advances in understanding of the dynamics of human behaviour are increasingly taken into account by moral theologians, who try to study acts of suicide with the maximum of individual and pastoral understanding, without, objectively speaking, belittling the objective seriousness of the act of suicide taken on its own. The pastoral aim is to seek the salvation of the suicide as far as possible, taking account of the personal conditioning factors that led him or her to carry out an objectively abominable act. This attitude of pastoral understanding is reflected in the canonical discipline of the new 1983 *Codex*, in accordance with the spirit and guidelines of the second Vatican Council.

2. SUICIDE IN THE BIBLE

The Old Testament gives some examples of direct suicide. Abimelech calls on his armour-bearer to kill him so that no one can say of him that he was killed by a woman (who threw a millstone down on his head) (Judges 9:53–54). Saul killed himself by falling on the point of his sword so that it could not be said that he had been killed by uncircumcised men (1 Sam. 31:3–5). His armour-bearer, seeing him die, likewise killed himself by falling on his own sword. Ahithophel strangled himself simply because he saw that his advice had not been followed (2 Sam. 17:23). Zimri, seeing that his town of Tirzah had been captured, set fire to the royal palace and burnt himself to death in it (1 Kings 16:18). Samson procured his own death together with that of three thousand Philistine men and women simply as an act of vengeance (Judges 16:27–30). Eleazar sacrificed himself beneath a royally caparisoned elephant (1 Macc. 6:42–46). Razis, known as the father of the Jews, committed a famous and terrible suicide: rather than fall into the hands of Nicanor, he threw himself on his sword, but missed his aim in the heat of the battle, climbed up on to a wall and threw himself off, but survived this too and finally tore out his own entrails and threw them among the enemy with both hands (2 Macc. 14:37–46). The only case of direct suicide related in the New Testament is that of Judas Iscariot, who, filled with remorse at having betrayed Jesus, went out and hanged himself (Matt. 27:5; Acts 1:18).

It is generally held that Mosaic law made no express ordinance against suicide because it held it to be included under the general condemnation of homicide. The Israelites held life to be sacred. Ancient Jewish morality had no place for suicide. However hard and sad life might be, there was never sufficient reason to curse God or take one's own life. Job's witness is eloquent testimony to this. Even the pessimistic outlook of Qoheleth, as seen in Ecclesiastes, gives no grounds for thinking that suicide can be an acceptable option. It is true that the Old Testament relates cases of suicide without adding personal condemnations of those who practised them. It is even said of Ahithophel that he was buried in the tomb of his father. But neither can it be said that these human touches imply an implicit approval of suicidal behaviour. Flavius Josephus, in *De bello judaico*, III, 8, 5, holds forth to his irritated compatriots against possible temptation to commit suicidal acts, saying that the genuinely Jewish mentality is hostile to suicide. Josephus goes on to say that the body of a suicide should be buried after sunset, and he expresses his contempt for those who consciously and deliberately take their own lives, although the rabbi Eleazar allows that help and human consolation may be given to failed suicides.

The general view of moral theologians, sketched out by St Augustine and filled in by St Thomas, is that the Bible relates certain cases of direct suicide as accomplished historical facts, but in no way indicates approval of them. There are also other cases of indirect suicide, or suicide in good faith, not discounting the possibility that some of their protagonists may have felt themselves to be divinely inspired to kill themselves. Direct suicide is always seen as an infringement of the fifth commandment of the Decalogue, which formally condemns homicide. According to Deuteronomy 32:39, God alone can deal in life and death. In Genesis 9:5–6, God will demand an account of every man's life. Ultimately, man is made in the image of God, and this is the root of his dignity. The case of Judas is told, in both Matthew and Acts, as the logical outcome of the treachery of the faithless disciple. But the description of his suicide also carries overtones of evident repugnance for the act itself. God's sovereignty over all human life is also affirmed by St Paul in Romans 14:7–8: 'The life and death of each of us has its influence on others; if we live, we live for the Lord, and if we die, we die for the Lord, so that alive or dead we belong to the Lord'.

3. THE POSITION OF EARLY CHRISTIAN WRITERS

The early Christian writers reacted against Roman suicidal mentality and practice. For Lactantius, suicide is something infamous and detestable. He equates the objective evil of suicide with that of murder. In a certain sense, the evil attaching to suicide can be said to be even greater, since we do not come to life through our own will but God calls us into life as his stewards of it. This is why we have to remain in the life we have been given and not abandon it till God ordains otherwise. He harshly criticises the philosophers and other distinguished figures of Greece and Rome who favoured suicide, calling it a morally execrable crime. In effect, all suicides are homicides, and the act of killing oneself is self-murder.[1]

St John Chrysostom warns against the possible temptation to bring forward the advent of eternal life through deciding to end one's present life. The future life promised to mankind must not be anticipated by thinking of its priority over life in this world. We must wait for it with anticipation, but first go through natural death according to the course of nature without ourselves bringing about the end of our natural lives. No one is permitted to take his own life against the will of God.[2] St Jerome is implacable in speaking of Judas: to the crime of betraying Jesus he added the crime of hanging himself.[3]

On the other hand, while the position of the early Christian writers on suicide is solid on the level of principle, Eusebius of Caesarea relates some cases that deserve special consideration. All these took place in a context of implacable persecution of Christians. The aged Apollonia, after being oppressed and tortured, was threatened with death if she did not give way to the impious suggestions of her torturers. So, according to Eusebius, she asked for time to think, and, 'as soon as she was left alone, threw herself with a great leap into the flames, which completely consumed her'.[4] Speaking of the persecution of the Christians of Nicomedia, he writes: 'A tradition tells that at that time many men and women jumped of their own accord into the fire with unspeakable divine fervour'.[5] Describing the frightful torments to which the Christians of Egypt were subjected, he notes that some of them 'bravely held their heads out to those who cut them off'.[6] He also tells the case of a mother and her daughters who, fearful of being raped by the soldiers who were escorting them, opted for 'flight to the Lord' by throwing themselves into a torrent and drowning.[7] The tortures to which Christians were subjected were horrifying: 'Some of them', Eusebius continues 'to avoid torture, before being seized and placed in the hands of the conspirators, threw themselves off the roofs of their houses, considering death as a means of avoiding the evil doings of the impious'.[8]

These and other cases, such as that of St Pelagia, who took her own life rather than fall into the hands of her tormentor, have given rise to the view that the early Church placed suicide for religious motives on a par with martyrdom. This is completely untrue. As Eusebius admits, the only source for the cases mentioned is oral tradition, collected by Eusebius and given literary ornamentation by some of the Fathers, which in turn has produced the view that all such happenings are no more than a beautiful story. I should think that such cases are perfectly believable and that it is not difficult to regard them as having actually happened in view of the mentality of the early Christians who underwent such frightful persecution. What can be difficult to understand on the academic theological level can more easily be grasped on the level of popular faith. In some cases the Fathers excused this form of suicide and even praised it. St John Chrysostom, for example, wrote two fine homilies in which he sings the praises of Christian martyrdom, including that of St Pelagia, while making a very important qualification. St John Chrysostom presumes such a suicide to have been carried out *'nutu divino'*, that is, a result of supposed divine inspiration, to which the presumed martyr responded with an act of heroic obedience to the absolute will of the One who gives life and death. Given this hypothesis, such an act cannot be called suicide in the sense of a proud decision over one's own life in the Stoic manner. This morally generous and understanding attitude is also taken by St Ambrose.[9] The Fathers were benevolent when it came to judging the *subjective* motives of such Christians, whose sincerity in faith was beyond doubt, but was conditioned in their daily lives by their terror of persecution and an understandable theological ingenuousness. This understanding attitude shown by some of the Fathers cannot be taken as indicating that the early Church approved a sort of religious suicide as comparable to Christian martyrdom.[10] This can be seen even more clearly in St Augustine.

4. AUGUSTINE'S MORAL TEACHING ON SUICIDE

St Augustine treats the question of suicide with fine irony and even bad temper. The Donatists with their practice of suicide, inspired by ignoble religious motives, made him lose his cool. He sees every suicide as an objective murder. The cases related in the Old Testament have no moral force in the

New. Such suicidal episodes are related as historical events which happened, but which are to be condemned in themselves. They fall into the class of events narrated in Scripture so that they can be judged, not so that they may be imitated.[11] There is no pretext by which suicide can be justified, not even for the avoidance of sin or in order to put an end to a painful and unfortunate life. Those who toy with the idea of suicide with the excuse of safeguarding virginity and other ethical virtues, he castigates as fools and madmen.[12] Suicide cannot be seen as an act of Christian fortitude, but rather as a lack of it, since fortitude 'has the characteristic function of guiding and strengthening man in adversity'.[13] But what, he asks, is to be said of those holy women who, to save themselves from being violated by their torturers, threw themselves into the river? Augustine admits that the Church has honoured them, but displays considerable caution and reserve on the issue. If what tradition teaches about such women is correct, their recognition by the Church would be justified if they had some extraordinary reason, such as the intervention of some special inspiration on the part of God, by virtue of which these material suicides could be judged morally as acts of heroic obedience to the Almighty. Such a possibility cannot be entirely discounted, but Augustine is doubtful about whether it would have applied in the cases related, which had been handed down by oral tradition to Eusebius of Caesarea.[14]

Leaving such cases aside, anyone who consciously and deliberately takes his or her life is always culpable. Those who plot against their own lives despoil themselves of moral innocence in advance so that, when they die, they do not die innocent, but guilty of the act they bring about.[15] As we have seen, Augustine admits the possibility of a strange command from God which might have to be obeyed at the cost of taking one's own life, but he adds with heavy irony that if anyone is sure of having received such a command from God, then he had better kill himself. And who can boast of such certainty? He lists all sorts of mental disturbances and false religiosity as excuses for putting suicidal ideas into practice, but concludes emphatically: 'What we state, what we stress, what we demonstrate in a thousand ways, is that no one should voluntarily take his own life in order to free himself from temporal suffering, since he will fall into eternal sufferings; nor to avoid the sins of others, since then he—who was not stained by the sins of others—commits a most grave sin himself; nor on account of his own past sins, since if he is to expiate these through doing penance, he has particular need of this life in which to do that penance; nor through desire for a better life waiting for him after death, since there is no better life waiting for suicides'.[16]

5./ SUICIDE ACCORDING TO ST THOMAS

St Thomas, with Aristotle as his guide, makes Augustine's thesis more scientific and more systematic. The fifth commandment of the Decalogue is valid for everyone without exception, and that includes ourselves. Suicide is contrary to the natural law by which every one seeks his own conservation in life and resists any violent movement against the natural desire of life. It is therefore a direct attack on the love which everyone owes to him or herself. Consequently, suicide is a mortal sin. Following Aristotle, he also uses the argument of the whole and the parts. Each part as a part belongs to the whole; each person forms part of the human community and therefore, when someone commits suicide, he commits an offence against the community to which he belongs. Finally, he adds the strongest argument against suicide, which is the theological one. Human life, he argues, is a gift given to man by God and absolutely dependent on the One who, according to Deuteronomy 32:39, alone can deal in life and death. Therefore, anyone who deliberately takes his own life sins against God himself. The conscious and willed suicide, in destroying his own life, usurps God's power of judgment in a cause which is outside his (the suicide's) competence.[17]

Even when St Thomas allows the moral legitimacy of the death penalty (mistakenly in my view, as I have shown elsewhere) applied to certain classes of criminal on behalf of the supreme authority of the State, he denies that those who hold this authority can apply it to themselves.[18] Neither does he allow the argument from the autonomy of personal freedom as a pretext for justifying suicide. Man can dispose freely of his person in many things; but he can never morally decide his final transition from this life to another, happier one. Such a decision goes beyond the limits of human freedom and has to remain dependent on the will of God. As St Augustine said, we have to *wait*, respecting the course of nature, for the happy future life that God has promised to those who are faithful to him. It is never permissible for man to anticipate it by taking his own life.

St Thomas equally rejects sentimental motives like taking one's life in order to free oneself from the sorrows of this life on earth. Death, he says, is the last and greatest evil that man can suffer. So committing suicide is equivalent to choosing the worst evil of all. Nor does it make sense to take one's life to make up for some crime committed, and still less through fear of committing some serious crime in the future. Those who have sinned should do penance. If they take their life, all they achieve is to add another even more serious sin and remove the very possibility of penitence and conversion. Fear of future sins is a very weak argument. First, because, as St Paul says (Rom. 3:5), one may not do evil that good may come of it; the bad means cannot lead to good ends.

Now suicide is a great and certain evil; future sins, on the other hand, will always be lesser and uncertain evils. Furthermore, God is powerful and merciful in helping us not to fall into temptation and in forgiving us if we do fall.

On the suicides related in the Bible and the cases of persecuted Christians who took their lives in order to save their honour, St Thomas adopts the same reserved and unenthusiastic stand as St Augustine. The metaphysical possibility that some may have acted under divine inspiration cannot be discounted, but such a possibility in no way invalidates the arguments advanced against suicide in general.

Finally, St Thomas denies that suicide can ever be an act of real courage. Not even those cases described with some narrative enthusiasm in the Bible. He states that, on the contrary, every suicide supposes a weakening of human will power, which flinches at and gives way to the difficulties of life.[19]

6. SUICIDE IN THE CURRENT TEACHING OF THE MAGISTERIUM

The moral question of suicide comes up currently in connection with the problem of euthanasia, on which there is a recent declaration by the Sacred Congregation for the Doctrine of the Faith. This document, published on 5 July 1980, contains the following paragraph:

> Every person has the duty to conform his or her life with God's plan. Life has been given as a good which should produce its fruits here on earth, but which finds its full perfection only in eternal life. Voluntary death, that is suicide, is consequently as unacceptable as murder; such an act on the part of man in effect constitutes a rejection of God's sovereignty and of his loving plan. Furthermore, suicide is often a rejection of love for oneself, a negation of the natural aspiration to life, a renunciation of one's duties of justice and charity to one's neighbour, towards the various communities one lives in and towards the whole of society. Sometimes, as we know, psychological factors can intervene to attenuate or even remove responsibility. One should, however, draw a distinction between suicide and that sacrifice by which, for a higher cause—such as the glory of God, the salvation of souls or the service of the brethren—one's own life is offered or placed in danger.[20]

The document then goes on to refer directly to euthanasia, which it defines thus: 'By euthanasia is meant an action or omission which by its nature, or in intention, causes death, with the aim of eliminating any suffering'. And it adds that, 'it is necessary to state with all firmness that nobody can authorise the death of an innocent human being, foetus or embryo, child or adult, old person, or anyone suffering from an incurable or terminal disease. Nobody, furthermore, can ask for this act of homicide for him or herself or for others entrusted to his or her care, nor consent explicitly or implicitly to it. No authority can legitimately impose it or tolerate it. Such an action would, in effect, be a violation of the divine law, an offence against the dignity of the human person, a crime against life, an attack on humanity.'[21] As can be seen, euthanasia is equated with direct suicide, which is objectively self-murder.

7. CANONICAL DISCIPLINE ON SUICIDE

Christian moral teaching on suicide has always been reflected in canon law. According to the discipline laid down in the Canons of the Apostles, lay people who mutilated themselves were to be excluded from receiving holy orders. If they were clerics, they should be stripped of their office. Mutilation was seen as morally a homicidal aggression against life, which is above all God's work. From this explicit condemnation of mutilation can be deduced an implicit condemnation of suicide.[22] The Council of Guadix (305) contains an interesting admonition excluding from the ranks of the martyrs all those who for various reasons took their own lives.[23] Later, the Council of Carthage (348) condemned those pseudo-martyrs who, on the pretext of various personal motives, deliberately took their own lives.[24] When Archbishop Timothy of Alexandria was asked if the liturgy should be celebrated for those who committed suicide in a state of mental abnormality, he replied that those who asked for the liturgical celebration were often lying when they claimed that the suicide did not know what he was doing. So he told those who consulted him to be watchful in this matter, and that, whenever it was proved that the act had been committed deliberately, celebration of the liturgical offices for the dead was to be omitted.[25] The Council of Braga (563) was explicit and forthright: those who killed themselves in any way were to be excluded from liturgical intercession and taken to burial without the solemnity of psalm-singing.[26] In 806 Pope Nicholas I replied to a question from the Bulgars in these terms: suicides must be buried without the liturgical ceremonial usual in the offices for the dead. In particular, mass was not to be said, since not only did they sin till their death, but even gave themselves death. To emphasise the moral gravity of suicide and justify the canonical penalties attached to it, he referred to the suicide of Judas. Nevertheless, he did not exclude the making of certain humanitarian gestures during the burial of suicides.[27]

The *Codex* of 1917 imposed sanctions on suicides through its teaching that whoever consciously and deliberately attempts to take his own life attacks the divine right expressed in the fifth commandment of the Decalogue and in other places in Christian revelation. Consequently, canons 1240, 1, 3 and 2350, 2 forbid ecclesiastical burial to all those who '*deliberato consilio*', that is freely and with full use of their faculties, take their own lives. But this sanction was not to be applied to those who took their own lives under the influence of some defect in their human faculties, since the condition '*deliberato consilio*' could not be applied to them. In the event of doubt over the true intentions of the person committing suicide, ecclesiastical burial should be proceeded with, avoiding any possible scandal among the faithful (can. 1240, 2), and the usual pomp and ceremony. The refusal of ecclesiastical burial implied suppression of the requiem mass and mass on the anniversary of death (can. 1241). But masses could be said for suicides in private. In applying this sanction it was supposed that the dead person had not given any sign of repentance before dying. Where this was not the case, ecclesiastical burial should be carried out in the normal form proper to all the faithful departed.

Canon law showed itself no more lax in the *Codex* of 1917 to those who attempted suicide without succeeding. If they were lay people, they incurred an '*ex delicto*' irregularity, which prevented them from applying to receive holy orders without a special dispensation (can. 985, 5). Neither could they act as godparents at baptisms (can. 762, 2; 766, 2; 795, 2, 2256, 2). In the case of clerics, they were suspended '*a divinis*' for a time to be determined by the Ordinary, and also excluded from any office or benefice connected with the care of souls (can. 2350).

According to the Ritual for the office for the Dead, confirmed by the Sacred Congregation of Rites on 23 September 1971, n. 64, the Ordinary of the diocese was always to be consulted before denying ecclesiastical burial in cases covered by the law in force; he would determine what pastoral prudence determined as most suitable. What has been established in current canon law, i.e. in the *Codex* of 1983, is that those who have attempted suicide should be declared 'irregular' for receiving holy orders or for exercising them (can. 1041 & 1044). In regard to the traditional denial of ecclesiastical burial to suicides, canon 1184, without specifically mentioning suicides, speaks of 'manifest sinners to whom the rites for the dead cannot be offered without causing public scandal to the faithful'. From which one deduces that, in accordance with the spirit of the new *Codex* of canon law, the question of possible denial of ecclesiastical burial to suicides is entrusted completely to the pastoral prudence of the bishop, who will decide what is most appropriate in each particular case.

CONCLUSION

The Church still holds firmly to the traditional moral criteria against the mentality and practice of direct suicide carried out with deliberation and full knowledge. In disciplinary practice, however, canon law, reformed in accordance with the principles of the second Vatican Council, aims at a more pastoral approach. This is why it explicitly limits itself to excluding would-be suicides from holding or exercising holy orders. The traditional denial of ecclesiastical burial to suicides has been suspended, and the decision entrusted to the pastoral judgment of the bishop of the diocese, who will decide whether or not to refuse such burial in such a way as to make a public judgment on the act of suicide, which is always objectively to be condemned, while at the same time displaying the maximum of Christian charity toward and understanding of human weakness.

Translated by Paul Burns

Notes

1. Lactantius *Divin. Institu.* III, 18 in PL 6, 405–408.
2. St John Chrysostom *De consolatione mortis* in PG 56, 299.
3. St Jerome *Comment. in Math.* IV, 17 in PL 25, 1129.
4. Eusebius *Historia ecclesiastica* VI, 41, 7.
5. *Ibid.* VIII, 6, 6.
6. *Ibid.* VIII, 8.
7. *Ibid.* VIII, 12, 3–4.
8. *Ibid.* 12, 2.
9. St John Chrysostom *De sancta Pelagia virgine et martyre* in PG 50, 579–586; St Ambrose *De virginibus* III, 7 in PL 16, 241–243.
10. B. Alaimo, 'De suicidii nomine et quibusdam eius definitionibus' in *Antonianum* 31 (1956) 205–206.
11. St Augustine *Epist.* 204, 6–7 in PL 33, 941.
12. *De civitate Dei* I, 27 in PL 41, 40; *Epist.* 204, 5 in PL 33, 940.
13. *Ibid.* XIX, 4, 5 in PL 41, 630–631.
14. *Ibid.* 26 in PL 41, 39.
15. *Contra Gaudentium* I, 13, 14 in PL 43, 711–712.
16. *De civitate Dei* I, 26 in PL 41, 39–40.
17. 2a.–2ae. q. 64a. 5.
18. *Ibid.* ad 1um.
19. *Ibid.* ad 2um, ad 3um, ad 4um et ad 5um.
20. *Ecclesia* (1980) n. 1990 pp. 28–29 (1603–1609). AAS 72 (1980), pp. 454–455.
21. *Ibid.* p. 29; AAS 72 (1980) p. 546.
22. *Canones Apostolorum* 21–23, in Mansi vol. 1, 34.

23. *Concilium Eliberitanum* 60 in Mansi vol. 2, 15.

24. *Concilium Carthaginense* c. 2, in Mansi vol. 3, 153–154.

25. *Responsa canonica Timothei, Alexandrini episcopi* 13, in Mansi vol. 3, 1251–1254.

26. *Concilium Bracarense* II, c. 16, in Mansi vol. 9, 779.

27. *Responsa Nicolai ad consulta Bulgarorum* 98 in PL 119, 1013.

David Power

The Funeral Rites for a Suicide and Liturgical Developments

A PRIEST had thrown himself on the track in front of an oncoming train, to the shock of all who knew him and of those who heard the reports. Never had the diocese seen such a large gathering of people and clergy for a funeral. There was a great sense of tragedy because of the loss of a man admired by all and because of the way in which he had ended his life. The bishop presided at the liturgy and preached the homily. He read a passage from the dead man's diary, revealing that he had for some time contemplated this action. For personal reasons, he had found life untenable. The bishop passed no judgment. He asked the people to enter into the anguish of the deceased's mind and to feel the sorrow that enveloped his closing days. He reminded the parents of the man that they should hold in memory all the good that their son had done and assured them of the support and affection of the clergy of the diocese. To sustain the community's hope, he reiterated the belief in the lordship of Jesus Christ over life and death.[1]

Such a scene would have been unthinkable thirty years ago. The priest would have been buried hugger mugger, the circumstances of his death covered over by the veil of uninformed gossip. Today, the event cannot be seen as an isolated one, for it is no longer unusual to give Christian burial to those who have ended their own lives, sometimes even in circumstances more clearly premeditated than in the story narrated. Some Catholics may offer moral justification for suicide in certain situations. Most are probably still affronted and disturbed by it. Yet, while a few may still be scandalised by the Christian burial of a suicide, many are unwilling to pass judgment on the deceased person and deem it fitting to commend such a one to God's mercy.

1. CANON LAW

The canon law of 1917 forbade a Christian burial, or a mass of suffrage, to all who ended their lives by their own hands. Suicides were explicitly listed in the canons among those to whom ecclesiastical burial was to be denied. They belonged with apostates, heretics, schismatics, masons, the excommunicated, those who died in a duel, and those who had asked for their bodies to be cremated. The list ended with a catch-all phrase about not burying public sinners and avoiding scandal.[2] In the new code of 1983 this canon remains in substance, but the list of those to whom ecclesiastical burial is to be refused has been changed on several counts, reflecting changed attitudes. Particularly noteworthy is the omission of all mention of duellists and suicides.[3] While omission of the former may be only due to a sense of anachronism, the omission of suicides seemingly reflects an unwillingness to presume judgment upon such persons. This, of course, does not indicate moral justification of the act of suicide, but is more likely to express haziness about the psychological state and motivations of suicides.

2. THE MEANING OF CHRISTIAN BURIAL

To see the implications of giving ecclesiastical burial to suicides more clearly, it is necessary to look at the meaning of the Catholic funeral liturgy. This has in fact undergone considerable modification since the Second Vatican Council.

Before the liturgical revisions prompted by that Council, Christian burial was celebrated as an act of suffrage and absolution, having taken on this perspective in the middle ages.[4] Ecclesiastical authority exercised much the same power over the souls of the dead that it had exercised over them during life. The absolution over the coffin paralleled the absolution of the confessional. The priest's application of Christ's merits and satisfactions through the mass to the souls of the deceased was understood to be an exercise of ecclesiastical power, extending even beyond the grave. Theologians were wont to argue whether offering mass for the dead (as for the living) had an efficacy comparable to the *ex opere operato* efficacy of the sacraments, or whether it was to be understood as a plea in Christ's name to God's mercy, but few doubted the power of the priest to apply mass for the deceased in his capacity as minister of the church.[5] The use of this power and authority required that the Church's minister pass some judgment on the life and death of the deceased, just as the exercise of the power of absolution in the confessional could not be used without making some judgment on the sinner's worthiness.

The attitudes thus expressed in the funeral liturgy reflect a rather secure vision of the cosmos, in which knowledge about after-life could be based on knowledge about this world. As a person's participation in the sacraments of the Church could be based on a distinction between grace, mortal sin and venial sin, so the Church's ministerial relation to someone after death was bound to the threefold distinction between heaven, hell and purgatory. The Church was sure of the harmony between God's judgments and its own, relying much on the promise: 'Whatsoever you bind on earth shall be bound in heaven. Whatsoever you loose on earth shall be loosed in heaven.'

Morality had the same security, and whatever excluded a person completely from the Church's sacraments during life equally excluded that person from ecclesiastical burial. Heretics, schismatics and apostates were never supposed to set foot in church, alive or dead. The attempt on one's own life, if unsuccessful, did not carry the penalty of excommunication, but it was considered serious enough to debar a person from any ecclesiastical office for life, inclusive of deposition if one were already a cleric.[6] When the attempt succeeded, the Church judged the person unable to be helped any further by its ministry. To pronounce absolution over the coffin, or to apply the merits of the mass to such a person would have belied the Church's securities.

3. THE NEW FUNERAL RITE

The new funeral rite, which was composed after the Second Vatican Council as a part of an integral liturgical reform, centres in the hope of the resurrection and is intended not only for the needs of the deceased but also for the consolation of the bereaved.[7] The absolution pronounced over the coffin has disappeared, to be replaced by a final commendation of the departed to God. Of this commendation, it is said:

> This rite is not to be understood as a purification of the dead—which is effected rather by the eucharistic sacrifice—but as the last farewell with which the Christian community honours one of its members before the body is buried.[8]

In the prayer for the rite, the minister asks for a merciful divine judgment and the forgiveness of the sins of the deceased, as well as for a part in the final resurrection of the dead.[9] In those parts of the world where an unordained minister presides at funerals, this rite and prayer are still included in the burial service.

Rather than being expressive of totally new attitudes towards death and after-life, and towards the Church's relation to the dead, the introduction of this commendation into the funeral liturgy reflects attitudes in the process of change. Like much else in the new liturgy, it is not without ambiguity. On the one hand, there is a clear intention of removing any suggestion that the Church is giving absolution to the dead person, and in that sense pronouncing judgment in God's name. Similarly, the focus of the Church's hope is on the communion of all in the final resurrection rather than on obtaining a speedy release of the dead from purgatory. On the other hand, however, the insertion about the eucharistic sacrifice retains some of the old belief in the power of priests to affect the lot of the dead, by obtaining their purification from sin. However, this is now combined with an abstinence from any semblance of pronouncing judgment on the dead, and this is what is most important in the change from the old liturgy to the new. In other words, as far as the burial of suicides is concerned, celebrating a Christian liturgy in their memory implies no judgment on the morality of suicide, either negative or positive, but simply constitutes an act whereby the Church commends them to God's mercy.

4. THE ABODE OF THE DEAD

From what has been said, it seems clear enough that the issue of suicide's moral justification or reprobation is not at stake in giving Christian burial to one whose life has ended in this way. The extent of lucidity and responsibility with which a person commits suicide differs greatly from case to case, but all who were members of the Church during life can now be buried with Christian rites. It would seem, however, that these rites need to be celebrated with flexibility, and with recognition of the ambiguities inherent in the situation.

One of the complaints that has been made of the revised funeral liturgy is that it seems to be almost too presumptuous of the resurrection of the dead. In the effort to eliminate the lugubrious images of purgatory and judgment associated with the old rite, those who composed the new rite seem to have acted on the assumption that the dead person immediately reaches final participation in Christ's resurrection. The liturgy is suffused with an air of joy that is seldom muted, so that little room is left for the doubts and anxieties of the bereaved.

Culturally, this seems far from present attitudes towards death. The tendency in the Western world to camouflage death, to gloss over its reality and finality, has been often commented upon. This is but the counterside of uncertainty about what it leads to, an uncertainty shared by Catholics. We are far from possessing the sure knowledge of after-life that was common in an earlier age.

In the early Church, the martyrs could be assigned their immediate place in God's joy because of their witness to Christ given in their own deaths. The manifestly evil could be assigned a place in the lower regions of the universe. All other deceased persons were afforded lodging in a place of rest where they were to await the final resurrection. Some further struggles with Satan, beyond the grave, were envisaged before they could attain their rest, and the remembrance of the dead in the liturgy was believed to assist them in these struggles.[10] In the middle ages two things happened to this vision. First of all, not only martyrs but all the dead were deemed to have immediate access to the beatific vision, the resurrection at the end of time being reduced in importance. Secondly, the place of waiting was turned into a place of purgation. Thus the bereaved who had reason to fear for their dead, because of the incongruities of their lives, could be relieved of their anxieties by the belief in purgatory.

This easy cosmology no longer seems to hold, with the result that fears and anxieties risk being suppressed by the all too ready and facile hope of paschal joy. We could compare earlier and present positions on after-life by comparing a person charting a course by a map on which all regions are clearly marked with a person trying to find a way out of a maze. In a maze, there are false trails, deceptive indications, routes leading back to the starting-point. The person looking for the way out knows that there is one, but has to approach all avenues in order to find it. That is the game of being in the maze, and as different routes are tried out markings need to be made in order to recall each experiment. The person who succumbs to frustration and terror, and fails to keep account of experiment, is lost.

If the liturgy of the dead is to accept some of the prevailing attitudes of doubt about after-life, without losing faith in Christ's pasch, the question is whether it can be charted by a disjunctive rather than by a locative map.[11] The medieval map was locative. That is to say, the ritual and symbol of celebration could place each person, living or dead, on a clear map, in a properly assigned place, and the roads to the various places were clearly marked. All fear and ambiguity could be overcome in this universe by reason of the way in which the Church assigned people their places on this map, presuming this to represent God's attitude as well.

The disjunctive map would be more like the maze. Though some order is assumed, wherever a person is placed on the map there is no clearly discernible road to follow. The rites and symbols of a liturgy charted by such a map would not presume to resolve all ambiguities and uncertainties. They would rather set up a play between the incongruities and highlight the tensions in the vision of the universe. The acceptance of the unknowability of God would be as much its faith as recourse to the knowable. It would accept that finding the way to the exit would bring us into the mercy and love of God, while recognising that humanity's journeys were searches for that mercy and love. The bereaved would remember how the dead had struggled with the issues of life and death, had sought love and fought with despondency, and they would commend these struggles to God in Christ. There would be a sense that the living and the dead continue to search and struggle together, in the communion of a common hope in which all are involved in searching out the unknowable ways of God and of divine mercy and judgment.

It is within this perspective that in the case of a suicide a congregation can carry out the instruction 'to consider the deceased and the circumstances of his life and death and be concerned also for the sorrow of the relatives and their Christian needs.[12] In remembering the dead person, it is necessary to remember the struggle with life and its meaning that came to the final point of tension in death by suicide. Rather than focusing on Christ's resurrection, or on resurrection in Christ, the funeral liturgy on such an occasion serves to recall the death of Jesus Christ and his struggle with the forces of death, throughout his ministry and at the point of his own consummation. The solidarity of Christ with the human race in its struggle is more likely to touch the hearts of the bereaved than words about our solidarity with him in paschal joy. Indeed, it is only out of the memory of Christ's solidarity with human strife that hope can be born whenever the ambiguities and tensions of life's meaning are as prominent as they are in the stoy of a suicide.

CONCLUSION

We are living in a Christian age when the Church is more prone than at earlier times to recognise the limits on its own insights, sayings and judgments. This affects many areas of Church life. In turning to dogma, its definitive nature has to be combined with its reversibility, however paradoxical that may seen. In acclaiming the Lord's sacramental presence in the Church, the negativity of absence has to be embraced along with the comforts of presence. In making judgments in the sacrament of penance, ministers and congregations are aware that there may not always be perfect correspondence between binding on earth and binding in heaven. In other words, whatever the occasion, while much is revealed in symbol much is also veiled and congregations are learning to live with the uncertainty involved.

In fact, rather than creating doubt and confusion this ecclesial uncertainty builds a firmness in faith on the foundation of the image of Jesus Christ as

God's compassion. In the remembrance of his solidarity with the human race in strife and struggle, in facing the combat with death, there is the ground of hope. The funeral liturgy that is celebrated in the memory of a life that is ended in suicide is but a particularly poignant occasion whereon that ecclesial uncertainty finds its bearings through the commemoration of the solidarity of the body of Christ that was effected in Jesus's death.

Notes

1. For obvious reasons, name and place are not identified here. By way of contrast with the incident recounted, one is reminded of the story by the Irish writer, Frank O'Connor, 'Act of Charity', wherein the parish priest has a doctor and undertaker falsify a death certificate when one of his curates commits suicide, so as to avoid the scandal of refusing ecclesiastical burial to a priest.

2. CIC 1240.

3. *Codex Iuris Canonici* auctoritate Ioannis Pauli PP.II promulgatus, canon 1184.

4. On the history of the funeral liturgy, see Damien Sicard *La Liturgie de la mort dans l'église latine des origines à la réforme carolingienne* (Münster: 1978). For a comparison with the new liturgy, see Richard Rutherford, *The Death of a Christian: the Rite of Funerals* (New York: 1980).

5. On this theology, see Erwin Iserloh 'Der Wert der Messe in der Diskussion der Theologen vom Mittelalter bis zum 16. Jahrhundert' *Zeitschrift für katholischen Theologie* 83 (1961) 44–79.

6. CIC.

7. *Ordo Exsequiarum* (Vatican City 1969), nos. 1 and 18.

8. *Ordo Exsequiarum* no. 10. The English translation is taken from *The Rites of the Catholic Church* vol. 1 (New York 1976) p. 654.

9. OE no. 48. English translation, 1. c., p. 678.

10. As a good example of these attitudes, see St Augustine, *Confessions* Bk IX, 13.

11. See Jonathan Z. Smith 'Map is Not Territory', in *Map is Not Territory: Studies in the History of Religions* (Leiden 1978) p. 308f.: 'These myths and rituals which belong to a locative map of the cosmos labor to overcome all incongruity by assuming the interconnections of all things, the adequacy of symbolisation . . . and the power and possibility of repetition. . . . The dimensions of incongruity . . . appear to belong to yet another map of the cosmos. These traditions are more closely akin to the joke in that they neither deny nor flee from disjunction, but allow the incongruous elements to stand. They suggest that symbolism, myth, ritual, repetition, transcendence are all incapable of overcoming disjunction. They seek, rather, to play between the incongruities and to provide occasion for thought.'

12. OE, no. 18.

Jean-Pierre Jossua

'Life no Longer has any Meaning for Me'

1. INTRODUCTION: THE RANGE OF AN EXPRESSION

THE REALITY of suicides has always vastly exceeded the definitions into which religious moralists have tried to fit them. What was often no more than a psychological inability to go on dragging out one's existence has been taken as independent self-affirmation, or Promethean rebellion. What the actors sometimes experienced as a humble commendation of themselves to God, begging him to forgive and welcome them, has been condemned as an act of despair. But why should we reject even the despair of a non-believer of good faith when we teach that God is the sole decisive hope of human beings? Here as elsewhere, and without withdrawing any offer of guidance, it would be a good move on the part of Christian ethics not to treat any act as absolutely and universally good or bad in itself, in an abstract sense, but to inquire into its context, the possibilities available to the person who did it, and the meaning that was given to it—not its 'circumstances' but what it signified deep down.

In this issue of *Concilium* we are concerned with people who ask not to be kept alive artificially; who ask, indeed, that they should not be prevented from leaving existence voluntarily because old age, illness, physical or mental suffering, or a serious handicap, means in their eyes that 'life no longer has any meaning'. Here already· we have several distinct cases each of which would need very precise special treatment. But, as far as my own contribution is concerned, this complexity is hardly important. I do not have to make a judgment about the fundamental petition—other factors would have to be taken into account—but only about the reasons for it. It is·sufficient that it is always a matter of a circumstantial evaluation, made by someone on his or her own behalf—'for me, just now, life is without meaning'—and not of an unconditional verdict: that human life is absurd; or of a judgment made by someone else: that this child is too damaged, or that this old man is too far gone.

We can hardly hide the fact that, when faced with a formula like 'life no longer has any meaning', the Christian conscience is reticent and uneasy. Of course many people fear the possibility of a generalisation (such as might be made by a radical pessimist or an 'absurdist' philosopher), or an authoritarian deviation (if one ventures a judgment on another's behalf, then the threat of 'eugenic' suasions soon looms) of the kind that I have just excluded from the scope of my reflections. But if there is no question of anyone but oneself, in one's own particular situation, why is there still a problem? Is it merely fear of an excessively materialist notion of 'life'? Is a judgment involved that violates some basic Christian postulate: our relation to God, matters of evangelical consequence, or the religious meaning of suffering? Or are we to believe that if there is nothing more to say in favour of a providentialist, miserabilist and expiatory Christianity, then a bad conscience at the possibility of deciding on our own death because of a lack of meaning in the life imposed on us at present has to disappear along with it? I am inclined to think that the traditional objections, duly examined, could produce a more discerning attitude that would to some extent justify our hesitation yet prevent us from accepting a negative answer. Opting for a *possibility* is not tantamount to promulgating a law; no *point of reference* is an absolute criterion; and whatever may be lived *in faith* cannot be converted into a moral truth applicable to all human beings.

2. EVALUATION OF RESERVATIONS PROMPTED BY THE FORMULA

(a) The Decrees of Providence

'No one can say that his or her life has no meaning, because this existence, such as it is, was desired by God: it is from him that our ability to leave it comes, and from him come the events that have occurred; we can only worship his Providence, and submit to his will—it is he who knows the meaning of all that, and it is he who will take us out of this world when the time comes'. That is how many believers would put it now. It is also how almost all Christians would put it if we were back in the seventeenth century. At the close of that period, faced with questions posed by that way of looking at things when the world is seen as it actually is, some people either stopped believing, because of 'evil', or refused to admit that that was a valid process of reasoning, rather than a blind and profoundly disconcerting act of faith.

In the meantime a new finding gradually changed the context of the problem, and resolved the difficulty of faith confronted with 'evil' inasmuch as it rendered the argument with which we are concerned here more dubious. The development of modern science introduced a strict notion of causality within the phenomenal order. This made null and void the metaphysical 'causality' which included (first in Greek, then in scholastic philosophy) recourse to spiritual agencies when analysing facts of the physical world. Yet this metaphysical schema had been applied by theologians to the biblical belief in 'creation'. With God as the first Cause, it was the entire Stoic and not just the scriptural doctrine of 'Providence' which began to dissolve. This included all divine government on earth, in terms of direct or indirect causality. What in fact was condemned was the 'deism' which Christianity had given rise to in the fourth century. Very soon, as far as philosophers and scientists were concerned, but much more slowly for the general consciousness, it would be impossible to remove any individual fact, fortunate or unfortunate, from the phenomenal continuum of the universe and to refer it, directly or indirectly to the transcendent first Cause. Time and space themselves are co-ordinates which enable our mind to construct such a fact in order to apprehend it. What point would there be in isolating it and thereby reifying it? We have no idea whether it is the expression of the 'Will of God'. Even the question itself no longer has any meaning for us—which does not mean that God is not its 'Creator', as of all things, in the mystery of being, but in a way which is wholly mysterious as far as we are concerned and does not allow us to read into it any special intention in our regard. Moreover, there is reason to believe that a kind of animism remains effective behind the refined notion of Providence; an infantile attitude which consists in reassuring oneself while attributing protective or punitive intentions to things and events. Of course we do that instinctively in order to banish our fear of the 'chance' which is part of the structure of our universe: those random happenings which are not entirely the products of determinist forces or of intentional decisions.

Hence the body and the abilities doled out to us by genetic chance, the character forged for us by the play of emotional relations in our childhood and the riches or impoverishment of our social environment. Hence the events of existence which have produced the situation which we now are in, and will be in until we die. If it is true to say of them as of the universe as a whole that we can accept them all from the hand of God in the action of grace, or bombard him with our objections about the unjustifiably excessive evil that they sometimes comprise, it is no less true that we cannot attribute them to his individual 'Will' or opine that they must all have a meaning in every instance. This certainly amounts to a Copernican revolution in the religious order which accords with the mental changes accompanying the growth of the modern world. Admittedly this loss of direct reference to God in natural events (and, it must be added, in historical events) is also a great affliction.

However, the God of twentieth-century Christians is not the God of Epicurus: a God uninterested in human affairs, 'paring his finger-nails' in the Empyrean. For the relationship which God entered into with human beings, according to the message of the prophets and Jesus Christ, is so profound that it can survive any such change. To be sure, the Bible tells us of the direct dependence of events on God, but on the one hand there is no question of a providential order which would explain evil (but rather of unforeseen interventions by a Living Being); and on the other hand that is not his most decisive contribution. What this tells us essentially is that there is no situation in which God cannot reach us and which he cannot experience with us, whether it is produced by the hazards of existence or through our own fault. More than that: he summons us from the depths of this situation and awaits us there in order to be our future, enabling us to *endow it with meaning* through faith in him and the hope which he opens up to us. Hence we may understand *both* that it is impossible to obtain from our relation to God any unconditional statement of meaning regarding our situation, along with an absolute prohibition of laying down the burden which has become too much for our strength; *and* that by generalising such a resort too easily we may forgo a chance to receive our God and to be received by him *here and now*, in order to draw from him the strength still to endure this hour in peace and give it a meaning. In this perspective we may understand that only a living Christian faith can look out from such a viewpoint. We may also see that we can only hear non-believing friends out with total respect as they evaluate their possibilities of life and define the criteria of meaning which enable them to reach a decision. 'It was he who created man in the beginning, and he left him in the power of his own Counsel' (Sir. 15:14).

(b) The Right Use of Handicaps

Evangelical instinct and reflection part company when faced with some serious handicaps. On the one hand, we do not wish on the basis of principles to condemn others to bear indefinitely a burden whose weight we have not felt ourselves. Medical science has increased the number of deadlock situations by saving lives which in themselves are wretched, at the same time as reducing that number by curing defects or ghastly sicknesses in viable human beings— and physical or intellectual handicaps are perhaps not the worst things here. On the other hand, the experience of lives which have proved unusually rich because they have had the strength to overcome immense obstacles and because they have been helped to do so, inasmuch as faith assures us that God is close to all human life and that it has value in his eyes at least, persuades us not to assert too easily that any existence (one's own or *a fortiori* that of another, which is to be abandoned when it meets with a setback) is lost, 'because it does not have and no longer will have any meaning'.

Against any condemnation of earthly existence and its success and happiness, and against the image of a perverse God who would humiliate and even destroy his creature in order to make it grow or to lead it to him by some crazy detour, we should remember that the God of the Bible desires the happiness of the men and women whom he has created; and that his stature is not diminished by our success but on the contrary delights in it. That should be the decisive perspective. We may be perfectly aware that there is no question of a naive vision of any human 'flourishing'; that life consists as much of trials overcome as of easy victories; and that to agree wholeheartedly to play the game of existence instead of abandoning it for some 'spiritual' reason means ultimately, and above all, facing its risks. All that changes nothing: it is the positive aspect that one aims at with God. But the Bible also privileges the unimportant and the simple; the news of the Kingdom offers comfort to the deprived. There is a candour and happiness of faith, an immediacy of spiritual experience, a mystery of freedom, which are not incompatible with the most impoverished and maimed states of humanity. All that is food for thought. A very odd kind of physics so to speak corresponds to all these intangible realities. They would seem to be able to exist whole and entire in the smallest space, and to be able to pass just as well through great open doors as through the tiniest area window most obscured by extreme determinisms and limitations.

This thought which, yet again, is secondary and almost 'marginal', helps to inspire respect for and to demonstrate the hidden riches of some lives which seem most impoverished—against any morality of the 'masters', in the face of which Christianity imposes a radical choice. It conduces to struggle to give everyone his or her maximal chances of physical, emotional and spiritual life, with a chronic handicap as in the diminished situations of sickness and old age. Here there is awareness of a possibility, but only of a possibility. We cannot be sure that it will be offered *in every case*; it cannot form the basis of a refusal in principle to assert on behalf of this or that individual, at this or that moment, that his or her meaningful resources are exhausted. To say that God *must* always make them *subjectively* adequate is not to take seriously the tension which exists for us between his love, in which we believe, and the observable evil which seems necessarily to give us cause to doubt it, especially when it affects not material conditions but spiritual resources which do not entirely depend on those conditions. An affirmation that *for him* they are always *objectively* fulfilled no longer amounts to human discourse for human beings, which enables us to ground an action, but to an eschatological hope for which we can only have recourse to the One in whom we have believed. However, these thoughts once again demand that we do not simplify things, and do not overlook any possible chance. This time, the open perspective, though formulated here in Christian terms, perhaps has greater significance. Neither freedom, nor the strength to hold on and be creative in limit-situations, nor spiritual life are exclusive privileges of believers. If this chance is given to others, perhaps for us it is not unconnected with our God whose 'kingdom' far exceeds historical Christianity and never ceases to come in all humanity . . .

(c) The Fruits of Suffering

I did not find it easy to exclude from the two foregoing discussions, for clarity's sake, one question which belongs there traditionally: the supreme value of suffering. This particular point has been seen as bearing so much significance and fruitfulness, by reason of its connection with the redemptive passion of Christ, that it has been seen as applicable to any seemingly wretched situation which has no apparent outcome. This was true even if one no longer saw the situation as sent by God as a punishment for sin and in expiation, or if one refused to see the handicapped person as drawing all his or her dignity from it. The idea of a loving God who punishes human beings through suffering, and the idea of so universal an extension of so profound a corruption of 'original sin' that only a radical redemption could heal it, were in some way essentially unedifying. And it was on the cards that one day history, exegesis, experience and fundamental religious reflection would bring them into question. But we have to go to the heart of the problem, to consider the very conception of expiating sin through pain and death, as well as the conviction that Christ effectively offered such an expiation to God for human salvation, and that it can be renewed in us subsequently for our own benefit and for the benefit of our neighbour: 'God is miserly and does not allow any creature to be illumined unless a little impurity is consumed at the same time, that of the creature in question or from round about, like the charcoal which is blown on in the thurible' (Claudel, *L'Annonce faite à Marie*, Act III, scene iii).

To put it summarily, a doctrine of this kind is grounded neither in the preaching of Jesus (for whom divine forgiveness is offered to the sinner directly, without any byways or conditions, with the assurance that he or she possesses his or her own resources in order to respond to this summons); nor in the theology which is to be found in all the authors of the New Testament, according to which the resurrection *is* the mystery of Salvation (so that in any hypothesis the saving value of the passion and the cross cannot be conceived of apart from its connection with resurrection); nor in the conception of sacrifice in the Old Testament; nor in the oldest understanding of the meaning of Jesus's death (as a martyr prophet, going to the very limit of his witness, without any expiatory intention). This understanding is maintained by Luke and John in full knowledge of the reason, and even though their Christology already recognizes the Son of God in Jesus. It is true that other New Testament texts—especially the Pauline corpus—contain later traces of Hellenistic origin. But they are difficult to interpret, and in any case they cannot mean that suffering or the spilling of blood *in themselves* possess a redemptive value which is not conferred on them by the Saviour's voluntary and loving gift of himself. Substitution properly speaking is never mentioned. It was in the scarcely biblical context of a religion of fear—stressing the aspect of the annoyed divinity who has to be conciliated by sacrifice—that these elements were later amplified in the patristic era. They were then unsystematically associated with other, different approaches. Finally, it was only in the twelfth century that the Anselmian theory of satisfaction began its process of centuries-long reduction of the meaning of the cross to the level of propitiatory suffering, by associating it with the Augustinian doctrine of original sin, to afford the pattern with which we are familiar. Nevertheless, other ideas, like that of divine compassion, revealed in the notion of the Son giving his life for his friends, and saving us as an absolute manifestation of a love which has the power to change hearts, or like that of the resurrection invading the world by virtue of its saving power and banishing the shadows of evil, have not entirely lost their hold even in the Latin West—the East never having known either original sin or vicarious satisfaction.

If this simultaneously kindly and angry God who has to send his Son to die in order to forgive sins in response to that Son's expiatory sacrifice, and the suffering of the kindly Christ itself, must both be consigned to the theological chamber of horrors, talk about our own sufferings cannot emerge unscathed. It is no longer possible to see them as co-redeeming efforts, or as *having meaning and value in themselves*. At any rate, if it is permissible to say that on the cross God-as-man descended to the level of the most profound human wretchedness—saving us by making God's love for us manifest to us to an extreme degree—here too we may find the solidarity which was contracted with all suffering humanity. We may be sure that there is no situation such that he has not touched it and that he cannot extend his hand to us in it. For the believer, *suffering may* begin in *assuming a meaning*, in changing significance. Henceforth we look in the face this suffering which is hated, denied and rejected by everyone. Indeed, there is no reason to love a suffering which so rarely elevates and so often degrades and destroys; instead we may *acknowledge* it. God can be found in suffering *itself*. This possibility, once again, this little thread of joy and hope which may run and sing through suffering is not the least precious gift of Christian faith to those who have discovered it. Once again we are invited not to affirm the presence of a meaning where it cannot be found directly, and where eventually it cannot be discerned, which means both accepted and created. Nor are we asked to conclude too quickly a deficiency of meaning where it is still possible for us to supply one. Once again, as in the initial stage of this article, we have happened on a form of discourse which is meaningful only to believers, even if they are allowed to believe that this solidarity with all misery which God established in Christ transcends that misery with a promise which is certainly inconceivable but by no means ludicrous.

3. CONCLUSION

It would seem to me, in conclusion, that the reservations permissible for the Christian conscience when faced with the formula 'life no longer has any meaning for me'—inasmuch as it runs the risk of losing the chance to experience with dignity, hope and the nearness of God situations which seem henceforth to offer only failure and absurdity—do not allow us to assert that a loyal believer, and more justifiably a non-believer, can never be reduced to such an assertion. It may be called for to express the fact that their sufferings and those of people round about are becoming intolerable, and any possible positive in their existence is becoming null and void. To be sure, before passing final judgment believer and unbeliever alike must ask whether their conception of 'life' itself has given sufficient prominence to, or has at least included, spiritual riches which remain even when other resources are exhausted. Of course, a believer has to experience this standpoint before and with God as much as before his own self, but in so doing all he or she has to refer to is that love which is the 'fulfilling of the law' (Rom. 13:10). There is no need for any further reference, it seems to me, for the points which I have looked at in this article.

Adrian Holderegger

A Right to a Freely Chosen Death?
Some Theological Considerations

1. THE CONTEXT OF THE PROBLEM

SINCE THE beginning of the modern age human life is increasingly experienced as something the shaping of which falls within one's own responsibility. To the extent that shaping the world and oneself is acknowledged as a task and freed from the world of inherited religious views, the question of one's own responsibility for one's death comes within the purview of man's responsibility for his own freedom. This is seen most clearly by advocates of enlightenment declaring the problem of suicide to be the touchstone of autonomous freedom, since part of what indicated human freedom was being able possibly to be free to die.[1] Beyond this rather theoretical raising of the question, the problem of suicide has gained an increased urgency only with the progress of science and technology in the field of the social and anthropological sciences, to the extent that from the practical point of view the possibilities of manipulation and intervention in human life have been multiplied. Under the impact of these possibilities human life appears as something that in principle is at our disposal, for medical experimentation has long since pushed back the frontiers of taboo. As never before man seems to have been freed from being at the disposal of fate and placed in a radical situation where he must decide for good or evil about his continued existence, about his physical and psychological integrity. This fundamental experience, which has surely entered into the general consciousness, arouses a twofold sensitivity—for the quality of life and for the limits of life. The first aims at benefiting life in all fields: health, the environment, human relationships, and social conditions. The other, as if it were the reverse side of the coin, is concerned with the question whether, if he loses his vitality, if he is exposed to unavoidable misery and oppression, man may do away with himself. In this sense the old ethical question about the justification of suicide has emancipated itself from being the kind of problem that involves a borderline case and is connected more imperiously than before with the question to what extent and whether it makes sense to maintain damaged or ebbing life when there is only a limited ability to meet basic needs.

In this context various organisations are pressing for a 'right to one's own death'.[2] Such a right is principally demanded against the background of a social situation in which scientific and technological progress may have contributed to raising the quality of life but has nevertheless left behind in many contemporaries a fundamental feeling of resignation or depression because such progress would ultimately turn into a barrier against the development of the individual's personality. In this context it is not just a question of whether someone who is severely ill or disabled can in the final stage of his or her life bring about his or her own death, but also whether the suffering imposed by society and the breaking of the will to live that results from this can justify the ending of one's life. Many are of the opinion that social conditions of life might generate a 'suicidal climate' in which suicide would offer itself to individuals as the one single possibility of rescuing their own freedom: suicide as the ultimate if also despairing way out, to save one's identity from all the pressures on it in an act of freedom.

For the most part discussions of the right to dispose of oneself are conducted at an abstract level. In the context of the problem of suicide the reasons and counter-reasons that are adduced often remain six feet above the ground and remain defective as long as they are not enlarged by knowledge of the pathological and tragic dimensions of the phenomenon of suicide. The very fact that those at risk of committing suicide have in general a different assessment of the question about disposing of oneself from those who are not beset by immediate thoughts of death warns us against alienating suicidal anguish with abstract arguments. Those at risk of committing suicide prefer to put forward adaptive solutions that would guarantee them the continuation of life, while those who are 'healthy' are much readier to give life up in an awkward situation. For the present, however, we can presuppose an awareness of insights into the dynamics of suicide and of the results of investigations into the social factors that lead to suicide. But to sum up briefly, the findings of empirical research show clearly that concretely in nearly every case there is no question of the man or woman who in freedom and clearly weighing the issues up casts aside a life that has become intolerable or meaningless. People who display suicidal behaviour are confronted with external and internal difficulties that are greater than average. As a rule they are in a situation in which paradoxically they would like to cling to life but cannot do so in the given circumstances. If these findings are applied to an actual individual case, then what must be taken into account is that responsibility can only be ascribed to the acting person to the extent that freedom of action and ability to reach decisions are present. Among other things this has compelled the Church in practice no longer to refuse suicides Christian burial.

On the other hand, a thorough and serious discussion of people's right to dispose of themselves is necessary even though it abstracts from the immediate conditions of action and places in the foreground the general aspect of the moral judgment of suicide. It can play a part in determining the climate of opinion and in the long term exercise a decisive influence on suicidal behaviour. We should remember that Goethe's *Werther* encouraged a number of young people to imitate its hero and that today commercially successful books, with precise details about the fatal doses of drugs, encourage people to observe in due course their right to commit suicide.[3] However one may judge such handbooks and invitations to imitation, they make it clear that they share in conditioning people's attitudes to life and influence the climate of suicide.

In what follows we shall make the central theme of our considerations the theological arguments that in moral theology are usually brought forward to deal with suicide.

2. GOD, THE LORD OF LIFE AND DEATH

In the study of ethics he wrote before the *Critique of Pure Reason* Kant said: 'All pretence disappears if one considers suicide in the light of religion.'[4] Clearly Kant had in mind the statement that ultimately the only argument against the right to do away with oneself is a religious one, that of God's absolute power as creator which bars man from taking his own life. Similarly the philosopher K. Löwith took the view that there is only one watertight argument, a religious one that 'stands and falls with the Christian belief that man is the creature of God, that he was given his life as a gift. In this case, but only in this case, suicide is . . . an impertinent act of presumption, an act of rebellion by man against his maker.'[5] In fact the tradition of moral theology has seen in God's sovereignty the decisive argument against man's ability freely to dispose of himself. The two other arguments brought forward in the tradition—that deliberate and free direct doing away with oneself offends against the commandment to love oneself and against society—are of secondary importance compared with the argument from God's sovereignty. This is not least because the inadequacy of these arguments' decisive force has long been regarded as exposed. How one values one's life—in other words, one's love of oneself—is concerned not just with one's physical existence but also with the entire moral development of the person, and this, as is shown above all in martyrdom, can demand the sacrifice of one's physical existence. Valuation of one's own life, however rationally intended, offers no adequate criterion for distinguishing heroic self-sacrifice for the sake of others from a frivolous and fatal gamble. As far as the other argument is concerned, the moral claims with regard to society have their basis in the moral claims of the person himself or herself, in other words in the person's capacity of freedom and rationality that are not constituted by society but remain directed towards it.

(a) God's Sovereignty—Man's Feudal Right

Alongside the two rational arguments that have been mentioned, most theologians see the real decisive argument against suicide in the following specifically theological argument. God the creator is the one and only lord of life and death. Hence man is not absolute master of himself. As a consequence man enjoys only a right of usufruct over life, not a right of disposal *in substantiam*. Anyone who takes his own life interferes in God's rights of lordship. This syllogistic argument can be regarded as classical. It is to be found in St Thomas (see STh 2a.2ae. q. 64 art. 5), important handbooks of moral theology (e.g. Mausbach-Ermecke, Lanza-Palazzini), and individual monographs. But, however concise and plausible the argument may appear at first sight, it appears questionable when looked at more closely in detail.[6] In part the prohibition consists of an analytic statement: not to possess any total power of disposal over one's own life means that one should not kill oneself. But the prohibition still needs to be given a rational foundation. It is easy to recognise that the real ground for the prohibition of suicide lies in God's dominion over man. But the weakness of this reference lies in the fact that we are using univocal expressions to talk about God's right of dominion (the ground of all being) and the right of disposal that man is not entitled to (the act of disposing of oneself). Prescinding for the moment from the problematic idea implied in this theological language of creating a relationship of competition rather than freedom between God and man, the grammar of theology forbids us to make direct inferences about man's behaviour from any of God's predicates. To put it another way, statements about God can only be transferred to man in an analogical manner, which means that no unequivocal ethical imperative or prohibition can be derived from them. If for example someone talks of God's love and links with this the demand to do the same, this must be translated into the categories of human solidarity and human benevolence. In our context this means that first moral criteria must be found in which what is meant by talking about God's sovereignty can be grasped as categorically as with the moral criteria that have been used to decide whether killing another human being is allowed or not. God's sovereignty turns out to be 'merely' a claim on man's moral responsibility. In the tradition this responsibility is worked out teleologically in all fundamental questions of conflict (apart from direct suicide and the killing of innocent life), that is in the sense of providing a rational justification by weighing up the values and evils standing in question. In this way the teleological approach was used to arrive at the ethical judgment on the question of killing in war, the death penalty, and killing in self-defence, as well as in cases of indirect suicide when death is not the end intended but nevertheless is the immediate consequence of the action undertaken, for example as with self-sacrifice for religious or ethical motives.

We may adopt a slightly sceptical attitude to those exceptions today, but they make it clear that the thesis that man's life is not at his disposal must allow of some limitations in the face of serious cases of conflict. In any case Catholic moral theology has excluded from its general ban on actions leading to death not only allowing someone to die but also direct killing in unjust assault (as for example combatants in war) as well as indirect killing that accepts death in pursuit of some higher value (as for example dying in someone else's place in martyrdom). What is important here is not the casuistry that is developed but the conclusion that this brings out the conviction that life is not the supreme good but can find itself in competition with other high ethical values. In principle moral theology is of the opinion that in the cases mentioned risking and sacrificing one's life for another value (freedom, for example, or justice) is at least not immoral if these values do not thereby lose their fundamental justification or are not severely damaged. We would now need to discuss in detail the circumstances and situations in which moral theology has reached a moral judgment among the goods and values in competition, and also the formal criteria 'voluntary', 'indirect', and 'guilty' that place considerable limits on illegally having human life at one's disposal. This is not possible here, and also not so important in the present context. The decisive conclusion to be drawn from our analysis of the argument based on God's sovereignty is that a moral judgment about suicide can likewise only be obtained by comparing conflicting values or evils. As we have explained, man's status as a creature and his claim to freedom that are implied by God's sovereignty only provide a 'grammar' for treating life responsibly rather than arbitrarily. They include the imperative to translate the reality of creation into action in a responsible manner. In this man recognises himself as something entrusted to himself and called to give himself and reality a humane meaning. Among theologians this fundamental insight has increasingly given rise to the conviction that there is no other way than establishing the possibility of killing or suicide as one given by the creator along with the actual power of running one's own life, so as to conclude that man has to make the moral judgment of the circumstances in which it is to be regarded as justified and in which it is not. On these presuppositions suicide cannot be regarded *a priori* as an action evil in itself (*malum in se*) independent of the circumstances and consequences: the fact of human responsibility leaves open the real possibility of suicide for morally responsible reasons, even if in actual fact it has yet to be determined whether a case of direct suicide can exist as a responsible deed.

(b) Man's Status as a Creature—the Limits on his Ability to Run his Own Life

Recently the argument based on God's sovereignty and man's contingent nature as a creature or his being defined by his relationships has surfaced from the field of anthropology.[7] It is said that man's essence and dignity have their ultimate roots in the acceptance of man guaranteed by God. The determination of man's goals does not lie within himself but in the God that turns towards him. Man's inability to claim absolute lordship over himself, not just in his moral and spiritual existence but also in his bodily dimension, thus finds its justification in his relationship with God. It cannot therefore be man's concern to free himself from this state of being related to someone or something outside himself. Even if there is a multitude of ways in which man has to determine and decide his own fate, his bodiliness is withdrawn from being absolutely at his disposal. The limits of man's ability to manage his own affairs are reached at the point where human existence as a whole stands in question. This is because man's moral autonomy is confined merely to the temporal and historical dimension of his existence and not to its abolition. Is this second form of the argument to justify man's lack of absolute power over human life conclusive?

It must first be emphasised that the theological tradition is right to insist that human dignity has its foundation in God's redemptive and liberating affirmation. This guarantees the inviolability of human dignity.

There is no doubt that life is man's most fundamental good and the basis of moral responsibility and human dignity. Nevertheless neither the dignity of man established by God nor the life that participates in this is a sufficient reason for solving any conflict of values that may arise, as for example between preserving one's own life and saving another's. Otherwise one would be faced with the impossible task of having to deduce from the description of the dignity of the human person provided by the theology of salvation a prescription of how ultimately life is not ours to dispose of as we will. On the one hand what theology has to say about the economy of salvation indicates that man's value does not rest on some empirical quality attached to him but on God's consistent relationship of loyalty towards man. Because this dignity has its foundation and justification outside man, there is no life that is not worthy of life: it is neither social usefulness nor ability to communicate that comprises man's dignity but, in strictly theological terms, God's affirmation of man. On the other hand, however, these statements must still be categorised in order to obtain information in cases of conflict about what can and what cannot morally be justified. But this is not possible unless one takes the goods and values in question, goods and values that again are interpreted theologically, and makes a moral judgment about preferences. Since immediate norms cannot be derived from the statements of the theology of salvation and since it is the conviction of the theological tradition that, while man's bodily life does represent a fundamental good, it nevertheless forms part of a scale of values, asking about the possible permissibility of suicide means 'asking about the good whose realisation could justify causing the evil of destroying life'.[8]

3. RESPONSIBILITY AND HAVING ONESELF AT ONE'S DISPOSAL

On the basis of the preceding theological and ethical considerations our starting point must be that the ethical claim to decide the problem of suicide by means of a responsible weighing up of the different goods involved is tied up with man's freedom, which theologically can only be grasped as determining itself and claimed by God. Such a procedure demands a prudent investigation of the goods and values in question and a careful weighing up of them that does not avoid looking at the legitimacy or illegitimacy of the various forms of suicide. We shall try to indicate at least an approach to this by using the example of suicide in situations of need or inadequacy.

(a) Suicide in Situations of Privation

The question of suicide in such circumstances, which is connected with the question of active euthanasia, is disputed. Theologians argue that suicide as a final paradoxical effort to establish meaningfulness when all alternatives are meaningless would be conceivable in cases when man regards himself as 'the ultimate' (A. Auer) or does not believe in the meaning given to life by the being we call God. In fact this kind of suicide as a result of misery and distress appears as the most radical means of creating a meaning for oneself, if only by escaping from a life one no longer feels up to. In contrast the Christian belief in creation and redemption guarantees every man and woman a meaning and value so that he or she ultimately does not have to justify himself or herself in his or her meaningfulness and dignity. Even when life seems no longer worth living it is still borne by God's affirmation and made meaningful. But then the question arises whether from God's affirmation that gives meaning to man we can deduce a ban on doing away with oneself. The fact affirmed by faith that meaning is granted has the character of a transcendental theological truth which has an analogical relationship to actual human behaviour with reference to what that ought to be. Even when from a theological perspective man's being is supported by the affirmation of meaning that is ultimately guaranteed in Christ's saving act, man nevertheless remains committed to the task of determining what is right and thus what is meaningful, particularly as one does not know whether the meaning one believes in, God's 'affirmation', is realised exclusively in the preservation of life. On the basis of these theological considerations one may be able to say that suicide is a culpable act to the extent that it is a deliberate revolt against and arbitrary denial of the foundation of meaning on which human freedom rests. Nevertheless the question remains whether there is not the possibility in extreme situations of distress of committing one's life to its creator.

As a result, even when we look at the problem in the perspective of God's action in guaranteeing the meaning of life, there is no other way beyond a responsible weighing up of the goods involved for solving the problem of suicide in situations of need or inadequacy. Those moral theologians who in this case too decide in favour of a judgment based on preference cannot find any real reason that would justify direct killing in the wake of mental and physical pain or in the wake of illness and humiliating circumstances. In his or her characteristics of reason and freedom the person is a moral value which always takes precedence with regard to such unpleasantnesses as suffering and illness because they are non-moral evils. To take one's own life 'in order to avoid other evils of this life means inflicting a greater evil to avoid a lesser' (STh 2a.2ae. q. 64 art. 5 ad 3). In fact no objection can be brought against the argument that no preference is to be given to non-moral evils as against the moral value of freedom, which is of course always realised within the limitations of time and history. However correct in the abstract such evaluations may be, they are often of little help from the existential point of view. While one thing that is necessary is the indication of a morally right judgment, the other is the agonising task of approaching the tragic element of sickness and suffering, and of the hidden nature of death, in such a way that from this one can be helped to overcome it. Here it is a question of interpreting and spelling out the Christian conviction that God's affirmation that gives life its meaning does not let the evils that oppress men and women culminate in the absolute loss of meaningfulness but continues to envelop them in a way that goes beyond our understanding. Here is to be found the specific material of a Christian morality.

(b) Working Out what it Means in Practice

From what has been said it is clear that what is specific to ethics based on faith can be formulated not so much on the level of ought as rather on the level of meaning. What do the limitations on life mean? What is freedom, which is always present only in the dialectic of self-determination and being the victim of fate? What does death's hidden nature mean? Here it is a question of helping meaning to prevail over meaninglessness. God's affirmation that gives life its meaning is not least a demand to work out the practical implications in a way that interprets the Christian history of redemption and suffering as an aid to mastering life. The ultimate and decisive factor is surely that the hope that God confines death within its limits commits faith in a collective manner against death. The essence of death is its necessary limitation of life. This fatal limitation is best circumscribed by creating conditions so that death, which is possibly freely to be chosen, does not have to cast its shadow in advance first. The real demand on Christians consists of creating such conditions in which it is verified that man does not have to gain meaning himself in a prematurely chosen death. Living, one cannot do enough against death so that it remains what it is.

Translated by Robert Nowell

Notes

1. See John Donne *Biothanatos* (London 1646, edited by J. W. Hebel, Facsimile Text Society, New York 1930); Montesquieu *Lettres Persanes* (Cologne 1721), included in the critical edition edited by A. Adam, Geneva 1954.
2. For example, the Scottish and English branches of Exit, formerly and since the Voluntary Euthanasia Society, were from 1980 and 1981 onwards handing out a brochure of this type to members aged at least 25.
3. See C. Guillon and Y. Le Bonniec *Suicide mode d'emploi: histoire, technique, actualité* (Paris 1982).
4. Immanuel Kant *Eine Vorlesung über Ethik* (edited by P. Menzer, Berlin ²1925) p. 192.
5. K. Löwith 'Die Freiheit zum Tode' in his *Vorträge und Abhandlungen* (Stuttgart, Berlin, Cologne and Mainz 1966) p. 278.

6. On this see B. Schüller *Die Begründung sittlicher Urteile. Typen ethischer Argumentation in der Moraltheologie* (Düsseldorf [2]1980) pp. 238 ff.

7. See A. Auer 'Das Recht des Menschen auf einen "natürlichen" Tod' in *Zwischen Heilauftrag und Sterbehilfe,* ed. A. Auer and A. Eser (Cologne 1977) pp. 19ff.; U. Eibach *Experimentierfeld: Werdendes Leben. Eine ethische Orientierung* (Göttingen 1983) pp. 28ff.

8. B. Schüller 'Zur Problematik allgemein verbindlicher ethischer Grundsätze' in *Theologie und Philosophie* 45 (1970) p. 12.

Harry Kuitert

Have Christians the Right to Kill Themselves? From Self-Murder to Self-Killing

THE CLASSICAL answer to suicide given in the Christian tradition—by Roman Catholic or Reformed Christians—has always been an unconditional 'no'. This datum is bound to make us reflect. It is, admittedly, a very clear position, but it is open to suspicion. Such mono-causal declarations are generally over-confident in the cause they proclaim and they usually overlook the complicated nature of the reality in question. This is certainly so in the case of the classical Christian 'no' to suicide, a judgment that has resulted in self-killing becoming a special class of crime. Self-murder, if the term is permitted as distinct from 'suicide', is another way of expressing this act and it also contains, by analogy with the word 'murder', a condemnation.

The question of self-killing cannot be dismissed so easily—that is something that has gradually come to be recognised. Reformed Christian observers at least have detected that there is a tendency among Roman Catholic authors to describe suicide as a form of sickness.[1] That is certainly a step forward, when it is remembered that it has for centuries been seen simply as a sin and, what is more, an unforgivable sin. The person committing suicide is in this way at least saved from the Church's and God's judgment. But it is still not enough or rather, the price paid for being saved is too high. By declaring that he is sick and therefore not free, the person who has committed suicide avoids being judged, but is at the same time dehumanised by being held not accountable for his action. There are undoubtedly suicide and potential suicide cases who are mentally ill and therefore not in a fit state to consider what they are doing and even less capable of being held responsible. But those who do not come within

100

this group should surely be accorded the honour, at least partly—in a sliding scale of one to a hundred degrees—of having acted as human beings, in other words, of having acted with a certain freedom of decision. Even if a person has reached breaking point in his life, he still retains fragments of that freedom. It is even problematical whether we ever control more than a few fragments! But leaving that question aside, we are certainly going too far when we conclude from a suicide or an attempted suicide that the person concerned is therefore ill.

It is only when we have made certain of this that there is latitude for claiming moral and religious responsibility in the case of a person who has committed suicide. Suicide cannot be an offence against men or against God if those committing it cannot be held responsible for their action. Hence the moral question: Is suicide without conditions permissible? Expressed in terms of Christian faith: Is the freedom to kill oneself—under certain conditions—included within the freedom that God has given to men?

I shall in this article reply 'yes' to this question and support my affirmative answer with, I hope, good arguments.[2] In doing this, however, I do not deny that powerful arguments can also be brought against this answer. The 'yes' (subject to certain conditions) in favour of which I shall argue below is also ambivalent. As in the case of man's right or freedom to kill another man, the right or freedom to commit suicide is something which we do not have, but which happens and will continue to happen as long as mankind—and the Christian Church—exist. It is for the most part unjustified, but there are sometimes good reasons for it. A hijacker is on the verge of blowing up an aircraft with several hundred passengers on board and we shoot and kill him before he can carry out his plan. Most of us would say that it is morally permissible to kill in such a case, even though we would insist that killing is morally objectionable. It is difficult to see how there can be good reasons justifying such an ambivalent action as killing others and at the same time no good reasons for killing oneself.

In what follows, I shall outline four arguments why, in my opinion, the Christian Church should take into account the possibility of good reasons for suicide and should therefore recognise that it is out of place to regard suicide—in the sense of self-murder—as a special class of crime.

1. NO UNCONDITIONAL DUTY TO LIVE

The first and most fundamental argument is that it cannot be proved that man has an unconditional duty to live. Attempts have been made to prove this, notably by Thomas Aquinas and Immanuel Kant, but their arguments are not convincing. Only someone who shares their view of man would be able to accept their reasoning. This becomes even clearer as soon as we include other cultures, in which ideas about suicide are often less rigid than ours (even though it is nowhere regarded as 'ordinary'). This is, of course, related to the fact that in such cultures different ideas about man's life and death prevail. 'Different' in this case does not mean better, nor does it mean acceptable. All that I mean when I refer to other cultures is that Thomas Aquinas' view of man, which was repeated by Kant in his own way, is one option, a normative image of man, with on the other side of the coin, as it were, certain moral rules that we have to observe if we are to conform to that image. Neither Thomas nor Kant prove anything with their image of man. They simply repeat their own moral teaching with the help of that image and vice versa.

More recent attempts to derive an unconditional duty to live from the value of life have also failed. It is true, of course, that life is one of the highest values that we have as human beings. But 'value' is an experiential concept and there are exceptions to universal human experience. Anyone not accepting that concept is, from the point of view of society, reacting abnormally, but he does not for that reason have to be confined to a clinic, nor is he by definition a sinner. The unconditional duty to live is quite without foundation. If it has a foundation at all, this can only be found in religion.[3]

I shall return to this question later. Here I will simply suggest that the violence with which the unconditional aspect of this duty has been stressed in the Christian tradition can be explained. If this duty to live were not in existence, man would be free to cease to live in certain circumstances. The unconditional duty to live, in other words, is a dam erected to protect man from his freedom to have control over his own life subject to certain conditions.

I have in the preceding paragraphs had a very good reason for speaking about an 'unconditional' duty to live and the possibility of self-killing 'subject to certain conditions'. It is quite possible to speak about obligations—as distinct from an unconditional duty—which a man may have with regard to his fellow-men and the world and which oblige him to continue to live, however strongly he is drawn to die. I shall come back to this too at the end of this article.

2. FREE TO LAY DOWN ONE'S LIFE

The fact not only that a man does not in the factual sense possess the freedom to give up his life but also that this freedom forms part of the glory of his humanity is in accordance with what I have said in the preceding section.

Bonhoeffer has said that a man would not be a man without this freedom.[4] When he made this statement, he was, of course, thinking of a man who was entering death for the benefit of others. Many men do not regard that as self-killing, but their judgment is based on an error. The simplest definition of suicide is the deliberate ending of one's own life, whatever circumstances, intentions or means to achieve this end may play a part in the process.[5] This definition does not contain any value-judgment, but value-judgments obviously have no place in definitions.

In the light of this definition, the offering up of one's own life for the benefit of others is clearly a form of self-killing and, seen from this point of view, it is hardly surprising that John Donne, who listed almost every argument that has ever been used for or against self-killing, based his own liberal view of suicide to a great extent on the way in which Jesus expresses himself—in John—about the freedom to lay down one's life. Donne frequently cites John 10:11 and John 13:37 and draws the conclusion that 'Christ's own will' was 'the only cause of his dying'.[6] In saying this, he was not saying that Jesus' death was a form of self-killing (as some commentators have claimed), but was asserting very positively that man's freedom to give up his own life is something that cannot be changed, at least so long as one does not, as a Christian, want to change the origin of one's own faith.

The reason for killing oneself for the benefit of others, then, may be love, but where does love begin and where does it end? A father may save his family from the catastrophe of his being bedridden for years and therefore from being reduced to beggary by killing himself. Is that an act of love or is it selfishness? What are we to say about the act performed by Jan Palach, who killed himself to express the ideal of freedom? Even the possibility, which is for us very remote, of suicide as 'joint dying' should make us reflect. Is it really so strange that one person is ready to undergo what another has to experience—dying—and is it not possible that one reason behind this may at least be closely connected with love?

It is not easy to give a universally applicable answer to these and similar questions, but one thing at least is quite clear: as soon as we recognise that there may be good reasons for self-killing, such as the offering up of one's own life for the people or for friends, then it is no longer possible to regard self-killing as a class of action that is always and in every situation objectionable. Each case of self-killing or attempted self-killing can then be discussed in terms of whether it is permitted or not permitted.

3. AN APPEAL TO THE BIBLE

Does the Bible not forbid self-killing? I can reply very briefly to this question. All that the biblical stories of suicide do is to tell us what happened. It is quite significant that they contain no commentary. For the authors, it is clearly a question of the 'facts of life'. That is what people do in those situations. There is no prohibition of suicide to be found either in the Old Testament (in which almost everything that is permitted and not permitted in Israel is contained) or in the New.

It is, of course, possible to say: There was no need for it to be forbidden in so many words because it went without saying. Karl Barth went further than almost any other theologian in this direction, admitting that there is no explicit prohibition in the Bible, but stressing that that absence is not bad. We should not be tempted to read the Bible as 'Law' rather than as 'Gospel'. The reader who keeps to the second does not require passages in the Bible to know that self-killing is fundamentally a rejection of God's turning in grace towards man in the person of Jesus Christ. That is how the Bible contributes to our understanding of suicide, Barth claims.[7] It is clear, then, that, like so many other theologians working in the Christian tradition, his judgment—a harsh one—was already quite firmly established before he had begun to read the Bible.

4. MISUNDERSTANDINGS ABOUT THE CHRISTIAN TEACHING

Several arguments against suicide are used in Christian teaching (to which Barth appealed), but, however valuable they may be, they cannot justify the Church's unconditional 'no' to suicide. In this section, I shall discuss only one of the most important of these arguments, according to which believers know that they do not possess their life, but God possesses it and they do not therefore have the freedom to deprive themselves of their own lives.

Bruno Schüller has shown that this reasoning amounts to a tautology rather than an argument: We are not free because we are not free (we are, after all, God's property).[8] To this I would add that we are all God's property, but that this datum is clearly accompanied by a responsibility for our own lives and those of others, even to the extent that, whether they are God's property or not, others can also be killed. Whatever further meaning the statement may have, it does not contain any directive for action.

This does not mean, however, that believers should not take very seriously the fact that they are God's creatures, that their lives are a gift from God and that they may trust in God's guidance of those lives. All these confessions of faith are very important, especially in situations of despair, and they can help to divert a catastrophe. Suicide is, after all, and always will be catastrophic. But is it the greatest possible catastrophe? That is the question we should ask in evaluating others' dying. That is also why it is not permitted to kill others. With regard to his own death, however, a person may come to the conclusion that it may be a catastrophe, but that continuing to live may be an even greater catastrophe. Or it is possible for him to regard something or someone as so much more valuable than his own life that he would be glad to die for it or him.

It is not forbidden in advance, then, to follow the way of self-killing. It is certainly possible to speak here of a parallel between killing another person and killing oneself. In both cases a catastrophe takes place and in both cases it is a question of whether the killing is justified. In both cases too, a justification is possible to the extent that we can say that it is not always not permitted. Quite apart from whether self-killing, even though it is done for wholly objectionable reasons, estranges us for ever from the love of God. 'If I make my bed in Sheol, thou art there!' (Ps. 139:8). Friendship with the Eternal One is eternal friendship and is not destroyed by death—nor even by self-killing.

5. A CRITERION FOR WHAT IS AND WHAT IS NOT PERMITTED

Are there any criteria by which we, as outsiders and therefore with great modesty, can and may judge whether suicide is or is not permitted? My answer is: Yes and they are very obvious and have to do with the fact that human life is more than biological existence. Suicide takes place within a network of relationships in which men and women are not only dependent on each other, but also count on each other. That is why dying is always a catastrophe and an irreparable loss. People should not inflict this catastrophe on each other unless they have good reasons that will aslo convince their companions on the way.

The woods are lovely, dark and deep,
But I have promises to keep
And miles to go before I sleep
And miles to go before I sleep

(Robert Frost)

I know no better summary of the objections that can be made to suicide than these lines. In the complex circumstances in which our lives are enacted, it is really no more than the offer of a helping hand. Suicide is always a mysterious act and all our reflections about it—including my own in this article—have a certain ambivalence. On the one hand, we have to care more for our fellow-men and especially for the more vulnerable ones, because our industrial society is incapable of producing that care of its own accord. On the other hand, we would also like our fellow-men to recognise and exercise their own human rights and to be respected when they do this. We want too to protect them from the catastrophe of suicide and at the same time not deprive them of their autonomy. How can these two factors be combined without any trace of ambiguity remaining afterwards?

The safest way for bystanders is perhaps to love deeply and in time. In that way, it may be possible to prevent those self-killings that are more attempts—in the sense of 'cries for help'—than real intentions to commit suicide.

Translated by David Smith

Notes

1. See, for example, E. Ringel *Selbstmord, Appel an die Andern* (Munich 1974).

2. A detailed justification of my point of view will be found in H. M. Kuitert *Suicide: Wat is er tegen?* (Baarn 1983).

3. This has been recognised by V. Eibach *Medizin und Menschenwürde* (Wuppertal 2nd ed. 1981) p. 441.

4. D. Bonhoeffer *Ethik* (Munich 6th ed. 1966) p. 176ff.

5. See, for example, T. L. Beauchamp and J. F. Childress *Principles of Biomedical Ethics* (New York and Oxford 1979) p. 87.

6. John Donne *Biathanatos* (New York 1930) p. 187ff. The original edition was published in 1632.

7. K. Barth *Kirchliche Dogmatik* III, 4 (Zurich and Zollikon 1951) p. 466.

8. B. Schüller *Zur Problematik allgemein verbindlicher ethischer Grundsätze* (1970) pp. 13–16.

Contributors

PATRICK BAUDRY was born in Paris in 1956. He is a doctor of sociology, and has specialised in studies of death and violence. His thesis was published under the title *Mort, violence et sacré dans la société moderne* (Paris 1983). He has also written on hospitals, martial arts and crime reports. He is currently working on the suicide crisis and its social implications under the direction of Louis-Vincent Thomas.

NICETO BLÁZQUEZ, OP, was born in the province of Avila in 1937. He holds doctorates in philosophy from the State University of Madrid and the Pontifical University of St Thomas in Rome, as well as degrees in theology and psychological medicine. He teaches history of philosophy, natural law and aesthetics at the Pontifical Institute of Philosophy in Madrid, of which he is a Director, and is a member of the Spanish Society of Philosophy. More than a hundred published works include studies on abortion (1977), the death penalty according to St Augustine, and human rights (1980), as well as 'A challenge to philosophy' (1982) and an introduction to the philosophy of St Augustine (1984).

LISA SOWLE CAHILL is Associate Professor of Christian Ethics at Boston College. She received her doctorate in theology from the University of Chicago Divinity School in 1976, after completing a dissertation entitled *Euthanasia: A Protestant and a Catholic Perspective*. Recent research interests include method in theological ethics, the use of Scripture in ethics, medical ethics, and sexual ethics. Articles on these subjects have appeared in American journals such as *Theological Studies, Journal of Religious Ethics, Journal of Medicine and Philosophy, Chicago Studies, Religious Studies Review, Interpretation, Horizons*, and *The Linacre Quarterly*. A book, *Between the Sexes: Toward a Christian Ethics of Sexuality*, will appear in 1985. Dr Cahill also serves as an Associate Editor of *Journal of Religious Ethics, Religious Studies Review*, and *Horizons*.

PAULA CAUCANAS-PISIER is sixty-two years old, divorced and has three children. She was director of a business firm and helped to do work in family between 1961 and 1975. She is secretary of the Association National pour l'Etude de l'Avortement, general secretary of the Association pour le Droit de Mourir dans la Dignité for France, secretary and treasurer of the World Federation for the Right-to-Die societies and a member of the Mouvement Universel de la Responsabilité Scientifique.

HEINZ HENSELER was born in 1933 in Aschendorf, Ems. He studied medicine in Münster and Munich and became a specialist in psychiatry and neurology, and a specialist in child and adolescent psychiatry. Between 1962 and 1966 he trained for qualification as psychoanalyst at the Berlin Psychoanalytic Institute. Between 1967 and 1971 he was registrar and consultant in the Department for Psychotherapy, and between 1971 and 1982 head of the Section for the Study of Psychoanalytic Methods at Ulm University. Since 1982 he has been holder of the chair of psychoanalysis, psychotherapy and psychosomatics and medical director of the department of the same name in the University of Tübingen. His publications are principally about the problem of suicide and the psychoanalytic theory of narcissism.

ADRIAN HOLDEREGGER, OFM Cap, a Capuchin friar, was born at Appenzell, Switzerland, in 1945. He studied theology, philosophy, and clinical psychology, and gained his doctorate of theology in 1977 and his *Habilitation* at Fribourg in 1979. He deputised as a lecturer at Tübingen in 1979 and 1980 and since 1981 has been professor of theological ethics at Fribourg. His publications in this field include: *Suizid und Suizidgefährdung. Humanwissenschaftliche Ergebnisse und anthropologische Grundlagen* (1979); *Il suicidio. Risultati delle scienze umane e problematica etica* (1979); *Die Sehnsucht nach dem eigenen Tod* (1981).

JEAN-PIERRE JOSSUA, OP, was born in Paris in 1930. He studied medicine, became a Dominican in 1953, studied theology at the Saulchoir, and took his doctorate in Strasbourg. He was professor and rector of the Saulchoir faculties until 1974. Since then he has been director of the theological training centre. Since 1970 he has tried in various articles and books to combine the experience of faith, reflection and an effective literary style. Among his books are: *L'Écoute et l'attente, journal théologique II* (1978), *Un Homme cherche Dieu* (1979), *Lettres sur la foi* (1980), and *Prière* (1983).

HARRY KUITERT was born in 1924 in Drachten in the Netherlands. After studying theology at the Free University in Amsterdam, he became a preacher, working in villages for five years and among students in Amsterdam for ten. He graduated in systematic theology in 1962 and since 1965 he has been a member of the Faculty of Theology at the Free University. In 1967, he became professor of ethics and systematic theology, in which subjects he has published articles and books, the three most recent being *Wat heet geloven?* (1977), *Een gewenste dood. Euthanasie als godsdienstig en moreel probleem* (1981) and *Suicide: Wat is er tegen?* (1983).

ANNEMARIE PIEPER was born in 1941. Since 1981 she has been professor of philosophy at the University of Basle. She has published books on Kierkegaard, Schelling and Camus, and on philosophical ethics. They include: *Geschichte und Ewigkeit bei Sören Kierkegaard* (1968); *Sprachanalytische Ethik und praktische Freiheit* (1973, ital. 1976); *Pragmatische und ethische Normenbegründung* (1979); *Einführung in die philosophische Ethik* (1980).

DAVID N. POWER, OMI was born in Dublin, Ireland, in 1932. A member of the congregation of the Oblates of Mary Immaculate, he was ordained presbyter in 1956. He is currently professor of systematic theology and liturgy at the Catholic University of America, Washington, DC, USA. His latest book is *Unsearchable Riches: the Symbolic Nature of Liturgy* (New York 1984).

NEW LIBRARY OF PASTORAL CARE

This series, under the general editorship of Derek
Blows, Director of the Westminster Pastoral
Foundation, seeks to provide both practical guidance
and a sound theological foundation for those engaged
in pastoral care in a variety of contexts. Authors are
drawn from the Anglican, Catholic and Free Church
traditions.

Paid to Care?
Alastair V. Campbell
Alastair Campbell examines the
moral ambiguities inherent in the
'professional' approach to pastoral
care and suggests an answer to the
question 'Is it possible to talk
about expertise in Christian love?'
£3.95

Meaning in Madness
John Foskett
'A vigorous and forceful contribution to the growing debate on
the proper relationship between
religion and medicine at the present time.' *Dr Anthony Clare*
£3.95

Letting Go
Peter Speck &
Ian Ainsworth Smith
Both the dying and the bereaved
need to be helped to 'let go' of life
and those they love. Two chaplains
show how the process of grieving
can be used constructively for
human and spiritual growth.
£3.95

Living Alone
Martin Israel
Being alone is not necessarily being lonely. Martin Israel shows
how, for a Christian, it may be an
opportunity for a fuller spiritual
life.
£3.95

Other titles in the series cover Marriage Counselling, Caring for
the Physically Disabled, An Introduction to Pastoral
Counselling, Learning to Care and Liberating God – Private
Care and Public Struggle.

1. (Vol. 1 No. 1) **Dogma.** Ed. Edward Schillebeeckx. 86pp.
2. (Vol. 2 No. 1) **Liturgy.** Ed. Johannes Wagner. 100pp.
3. (Vol. 3 No. 1) **Pastoral.** Ed. Karl Rahner. 104pp.
4. (Vol. 4 No. 1) **Ecumenism.** Hans Küng. 108pp.
5. (Vol. 5 No. 1) **Moral Theology.** Ed. Franz Bockle. 98pp.
6. (Vol. 6 No. 1) **Church and World.** Ed. Johannes Baptist Metz. 92pp.
7. (Vol. 7 No. 1) **Church History.** Roger Aubert. 92pp.
8. (Vol. 8 No. 1) **Canon Law.** Ed. Teodoro Jimenez Urresti and Neophytos Edelby. 96pp.
9. (Vol. 9 No. 1) **Spirituality.** Ed. Christian Duquoc. 88pp.
10. (Vol. 10 No. 1) **Scripture.** Ed. Pierre Benoit and Roland Murphy. 92pp.
11. (Vol. 1 No. 2) **Dogma.** Ed. Edward Shillebeeckx. 88pp.
12. (Vol. 2 No. 2) **Liturgy.** Ed. Johannes Wagner. 88pp.
13. (Vol. 3 No. 2) **Pastoral.** Ed. Karl Rahner. 84pp.
14. (Vol. 4 No. 2) **Ecumenism.** Ed. Hans Küng. 96pp.
15. (Vol. 5 No. 2) **Moral Theology.** Ed. Franz Bockle. 88pp.
16. (Vol. 6 No. 2) **Church and World.** Ed. Johannes Baptist Metz. 84pp.
17. (Vol. 7 No. 2) **Church History.** Ed. Roger Aubert. 96pp.
18. (Vol. 8 No. 2) **Religious Freedom.** Ed. Neophytos Edelby and Teodoro Jimenez Urresti. 96pp.
19. (Vol. 9 No. 2) **Religionless Christianity?** Ed. Christian Duquoc. 96pp.
20. (Vol. 10 No. 2) **The Bible and Tradition.** Ed. Pierre Benoit and Roland E. Murphy. 96pp.
21. (Vol. 1 No. 3) **Revelation and Dogma.** Ed. Edward Schillebeeckx. 88pp.
22. (Vol. 2 No. 3) **Adult Baptism and Initiation.** Ed. Johannes Wagner. 96pp.
23. (Vol. 3 No. 3) **Atheism and Indifference.** Ed. Karl Rahner. 92pp.
24. (Vol. 4 No. 3) **The Debate on the Sacraments.** Ed. Hans Küng. 92pp.
25. (Vol. 5 No. 3) **Morality, Progress and History.** Ed. Franz Bockle. 84pp.
26. (Vol. 6 No. 3) **Evolution.** Ed. Johannes Baptist Metz. 84pp.
27. (Vol. 7 No. 3) **Church History.** Ed. Roger Aubert. 92pp.
28. (Vol. 8 No. 3) **Canon Law— Theology and Renewal.** Ed. Neophytos Edelby and Teodoro Jimenez Urresti. 92pp.
29. (Vol. 9 No. 3) **Spirituality and Politics.** Ed. Christian Duquoc. 84pp.
30. (Vol. 10 No. 3) **The Value of the Old Testament.** Ed. Pierre Benoit and Roland Murphy. 92pp.
31. (Vol. 1 No. 4) **Man, World and Sacrament.** Ed. Edward Schillebeeckx. 84pp.
32. (Vol. 2 No. 4) **Death and Burial: Theology and Liturgy.** Ed. Johannes Wagner. 88pp.

33. (Vol. 3 No. 4) **Preaching the Word of God.** Ed. Karl Rahner. 96pp.
34. (Vol. 4 No. 4) **Apostolic by Succession?** Ed. Hans Küng. 96pp.
35. (Vol. 5 No. 4) **The Church and Social Morality.** Ed. Franz Bockle. 92pp.
36. (Vol. 6 No. 4) **Faith and the World of Politics.** Ed. Johannes Baptist Metz. 96pp.
37. (Vol. 7 No. 4) **Prophecy.** Ed. Roger Aubert. 80pp.
38. (Vol. 8 No. 4) **Order and the Sacraments.** Ed. Neophytos Edelby and Teodoro Jimenez Urresti. 96pp.
39. (Vol. 9 No. 4) **Christian Life and Eschatology.** Ed. Christian Duquoc. 94pp.
40. (Vol. 10 No. 4) **The Eucharist: Celebrating the Presence of the Lord.** Ed. Pierre Benoit and Roland Murphy. 88pp.
41. (Vol. 1 No. 5) **Dogma.** Ed. Edward Schillebeeckx. 84pp.
42. (Vol. 2 No. 5) **The Future of the Liturgy.** Ed. Johannes Wagner. 92pp.
43. (Vol. 3 No. 5) **The Ministry and Life of Priests Today.** Ed. Karl Rahner. 104pp.
44. (Vol. 4 No. 5) **Courage Needed.** Ed. Hans Küng. 92pp.
45. (Vol. 5 No. 5) **Profession and Responsibility in Society.** Ed. Franz Bockle. 84pp.
46. (Vol. 6 No. 5) **Fundamental Theology.** Ed. Johannes Baptist Metz. 84pp.
47. (Vol. 7 No. 5) **Sacralization in the History of the Church.** Ed. Roger Aubert. 80pp.
48. (Vol. 8 No. 5) **The Dynamism of Canon Law.** Ed. Neophytos Edelby and Teodoro Jimenez Urresti. 92pp.
49. (Vol. 9 No. 5) **An Anxious Society Looks to the Gospel.** Ed. Christian Duquoc. 80pp.
50. (Vol. 10 No. 5) **The Presence and Absence of God.** Ed. Pierre Benoit and Roland Murphy. 88pp.
51. (Vol. 1 No. 6) **Tension between Church and Faith.** Ed. Edward Schillebeeckx. 160pp.
52. (Vol. 2 No. 6) **Prayer and Community.** Ed. Herman Schmidt. 156pp.
53. (Vol. 3 No. 6) **Catechetics for the Future.** Ed. Alois Müller. 168pp.
54. (Vol. 4 No. 6) **Post-Ecumenical Christianity.** Ed. Hans Küng. 168pp.
55. (Vol. 5 No. 6) **The Future of Marriage as Institution.** Ed. Franz Bockle. 180pp.
56. (Vol. 6 No. 6) **Moral Evil Under Challenge.** Ed. Johannes Baptist Metz. 160pp.
57. (Vol. 7 No. 6) **Church History at a Turning Point.** Ed. Roger Aubert. 160pp.
58. (Vol. 8 No. 6) **Structures of the Church's Presence in the World of Today.** Ed. Teodoro Jimenez Urresti. 160pp.
59. (Vol. 9 No. 6) **Hope.** Ed. Christian Duquoc. 160pp.
60. (Vol. 10 No. 6) **Immortality and Resurrection.** Ed. Pierre Benoit and Roland Murphy. 160pp.

61. (Vol. 1 No. 7) **The Sacramental Administration of Reconciliation.** Ed. Edward Schillebeeckx. 160
62. (Vol. 2 No. 7) **Worship of Christian Man Today.** Ed. Herman Schmidt. 156pp.
63. (Vol. 3 No. 7) **Democratization the Church.** Ed. Alois Müller. 160pp.
64. (Vol. 4 No. 7) **The Petrine Ministry in the Church.** Ed. Ha Küng. 160pp.
65. (Vol. 5 No. 7) **The Manipulatio of Man.** Ed. Franz Bockle. 144
66. (Vol. 6 No. 7) **Fundamental Theology in the Church.** Ed. Johannes Baptist Metz. 156pp.
67. (Vol. 7 No. 7) **The Self-Understanding of the Church.** Roger Aubert. 144pp.
68. (Vol. 8 No. 7) **Contestation in Church.** Ed. Teodoro Jimenez Urresti. 152pp.
69. (Vol. 9 No. 7) **Spirituality, Pub or Private?** Ed. Christian Duqu 156pp.
70. (Vol. 10 No. 7) **Theology, Exegesis and Proclamation.** Ed Roland Murphy. 144pp.
71. (Vol. 1 No. 8) **The Bishop and Unity of the Church.** Ed. Edwa Schillebeeckx. 156pp.
72. (Vol. 2 No. 8) **Liturgy and the Ministry.** Ed. Herman Schmid 160pp.
73. (Vol. 3 No. 8) **Reform of the Church.** Ed. Alois Müller and Norbert Greinacher. 152pp.
74. (Vol. 4 No. 8) **Mutual Recogn of Ecclesial Ministries?** Ed. Ha Küng and Walter Kasper. 152
75. (Vol. 5 No. 8) **Man in a New Society.** Ed. Franz Bockle. 16
76. (Vol. 6 No. 8) **The God Questi** Ed. Johannes Baptist Metz. 156pp.
77. (Vol. 7 No. 8) **Election-Conser Reception.** Ed. Giuseppe Albe and Anton Weiler. 156pp.
78. (Vol. 8 No. 8) **Celibacy of the Catholic Priest.** Ed. William Bassett and Peter Huizing. 16
79. (Vol. 9 No. 8) **Prayer.** Ed. Christian Duquoc and Claude Geffré. 126pp.
80. (Vol. 10 No. 8) **Ministries in t Church.** Ed. Bas van Iersel an Roland Murphy. 152pp.
81. **The Persistence of Religion.** E Andrew Greeley and Gregory Baum. 0 8164 2537 X 168pp.
82. **Liturgical Experience of Faith.** Herman Schmidt and David Power. 0 8164 2538 8 144pp.
83. **Truth and Certainty.** Ed. Edw Schillebeeckx and Bas van Ier 0 8164 2539 6 144pp.
84. **Political Commitment and Christian Community.** Ed. Alc Müller and Norbert Greinach 0 8164 2540 X 156pp.
85. **The Crisis of Religious Langu** Ed. Johannes Baptist Metz ar Jean-Pierre Jossua. 0 8164 254 144pp.
86. **Humanism and Christianity.** E Claude Geffré. 0 8164 2542 6 144pp.
87. **The Future of Christian Marr** Ed. William Bassett and Pete Huizing. 0 8164 2575 2.

CONCILIUM

CONCILIUM 1984

DIFFERENT THEOLOGIES, COMMON RESPONSIBILITY

Edited by Claude Geffre, Gustavo Gutierrez and Virgil Elizondo   171

THE ETHICS OF LIBERATION—THE LIBERATION OF ETHICS

Edited by Dietmar Mieth and Jacques Pohier   172

THE SEXUAL REVOLUTION

Edited by Gregory Baum and John Coleman   173

THE TRANSMISSION OF FAITH TO THE NEXT GENERATION

Edited by Virgil Elizondo and Norbert Greinacher   174

THE HOLOCAUST AS INTERRUPTION

Edited by Elisabeth Fiorenza and David Tracy   175

LA IGLESIA POPULAR: BETWEEN FEAR AND HOPE

Edited by Leonardo Boff and Virgil Elizondo   176

All back issues are still in print: available from bookshops (price £3.75) or direct from the publisher (£3.85/US$7.45/Can$8.55 including postage and packing).

T. & T. CLARK LTD, 36 GEORGE STREET, EDINBURGH EH2 2LQ, SCOTLAND

Human Experience and the Art of Counselling

Edited by Marcus Lefébure OP

A new series of discussions about counselling between a doctor and a priest. This book follows the outstandingly successful and widely read *Conversations on Counselling* (1982; 2nd ed. 1985).

These new dialogues include such topics as the drag of the past and the pull of the future in life, the problem of power-games, and the frequent tensions between the demands of a social morality and personal growth. This book is certain to be welcomed and appreciated by those interested in the deeper issues of counselling, in spirituality and in the influence of Rudolf Steiner.

Paperback   £3.95

T & T Clark Ltd, 36 George Street, Edinburgh EH2 2LQ, Scotland

---

NEW FROM T & T CLARK

Luther: Theologian for Catholics and Protestants
Edited by George Yule

This collection of essays show the remarkable contribution Luther made to the understanding of the Christian faith and they focus on his basic theological concern about the centrality of Christ. The contributors include such eminent scholars as Basil Hall, Harry McSorley, Gordon Rupp, Ian Siggins, John Todd, T.F. Torrance, and George Yule.

Clergy, laity and scholars alike, both Catholic and Protestant, will be certain to appreciate this important book about the teachings of Luther.

Available from bookshops or the Publishers

T. &. T. Clark, 36 George Street, Edinburgh EH2 2LQ, Scotland